Worship Musician!

Presents

THE WORSHIP
BASS BOOK

THE WORSHIP BASS BOOK

Bass, Espresso, and the Art of Groove

Norm Stockton

Hal Leonard Books
An Imprint of Hal Leonard Corporation

Published in 2014 by Hal Leonard Books
An Imprint of Hal Leonard Corporation
7777 West Bluemound Road
Milwaukee, WI 53213

Trade Book Division Editorial Offices
33 Plymouth St., Montclair, NJ 07042

Printed in the the United States of America

Book design by Mayapriya Long, Bookwrights
Book composition by Kristina Rolander
Let's Grab Coffee and *Espresso Time* logo design by Tim Devlin

Library of Congress Cataloging-in-Publication Data
Stockton, Norm.
 The worship bass book : bass, espresso, and the art of groove / Norm Stockton.
    pages cm. -- (Worship musician presents)
 Includes index.
1. Bass guitar--Instruction and study. 2. Contemporary Christian music--Instruction and study. I. Title.
MT599.B4S76 2013
787.87'193171--dc23
                       2013021727

ISBN 9781458443212

www.halleonardbooks.com

To my astounding wife and incredible daughters—
for love, laughter, encouragement,
and serving as constant reminders
that my God is an extravagant Giver

Contents

Foreword

Lincoln Brewster

It's always a pleasure and a blessing when I get a chance to play with an extremely talented musician. There's just something about the interaction, the skill level, the iron-sharpening-iron effect, the intensity, the feeling that you are playing as one and aren't afraid to let the music take you wherever it may. But it's an even greater joy when that person I'm playing with happens to be one of the finest human beings that I know, a dear friend, and yes, even better offstage than onstage.

When I first met Norm Stockton, it was at the very first year of the Christian Musician Summit in Tacoma, Washington. I was sitting down trying to figure out exactly what I was going to do that night, and somehow the idea of doing some instrumental tunes came up. I didn't have my band with me and was trying to figure out how that would come together. Someone said, "You should ask Norm." I'll admit I was a bit nervous at the idea of getting up in front of a bunch of musicians and jamming music that hadn't been written or rehearsed, but as soon as I met Norm, I somehow felt like it was a great idea. We got together for a brief sound check with Will Denton on drums and hoped for the best. Now I won't claim that we were any good that night, but I can tell you that I had an absolute blast and also made what I would consider to be a lifelong friend in Norm. A couple of years later, Norm joined my band full time, and we made two albums together and toured together for five years. I can honestly say that I can't remember ever seeing Norm get angry. He's always in a great mood and always adds something positive to any room he walks into. He has an amazing sense of humor and is also a very Godly man who loves his wife and two daughters very deeply. He is a loyal friend and takes his mission very seriously.

Now I can't name names, but I will never forget the night that a dear friend of Norm's showed up to one of our concerts—it was a friend whom Norm had been praying more than ten years for. At the end of the concert, I gave people the opportunity to receive Christ, and I couldn't help but notice that Norm's friend, who was in the front row, raised his hand. I thought Norm had seen this, and so when we walked offstage, I looked at him and said, "Wow! How cool was that!" Norm looked at me and in his usual fashion smiled and said,

"What a great night." I could tell that he hadn't seen his friend raise his hand. I said, "Did you see your friend at the end?" He said, "No, why?" When I told him that his friend had raised his hand to receive Christ, I will never forget the look on Norm's face. He burst into tears and dropped to the floor as if someone had instantly pulled every bone out of his body. He sobbed and sobbed and said, "I've been praying for him for so long."

The reason I told you that story is simple. When a man or woman possesses great skill, it's just that: a skill. And as awesome as that can be to watch, to my knowledge it has never changed anyone's eternal trajectory. But pairing that with a heart like Norm's—humble, loyal, faithful, and with a passionate desire to help equip musicians worldwide—now that's something that will truly make a difference in people's lives forever. That's why you're holding this book. That's why it was written. I pray that this book blesses you, encourages you, and helps you to fulfill all that God has placed in your heart to do.

Norm, you are simply of the finest kind. I love you dearly!

Linc

Lincoln Brewster, an internationally acclaimed worship leader, is the Worship Arts Pastor of Bayside Church in Granite Bay, CA. He has performed and crafted songs that have helped shape the sound of today's modern worship while also climbing Christian radio charts. These include global anthems such as "Today Is the Day," "God You Reign," "Everlasting God," "Salvation Is Here," and "The Power of Your Name."

Preface and Acknowledgments

Thanks so much for joining me on what I sincerely hope is a very fun and illuminating exploration into the realm of the worship bassist. I'll be sharing concepts, exercises, and tools to help increase your familiarity with the instrument, as well as your understanding of effective bass playing in an ensemble.

As opposed to a comprehensive methodology for all things bass, this will be more of a collection of the nuggets—many of which were acquired through lessons learned the hard way—that I've found valuable for my own development as a bass player.

I've been playing in the worship environment since 1989 and am well acquainted with the myriad challenges encountered on Sunday mornings by bassists around the world. It can be both exhilarating and really tough. My prayer is that this book might inspire, refresh, encourage, and equip you in your music and ministry.

While this book focuses primarily on musical concepts, please don't interpret that as implying that these concepts take precedence over the spiritual and heart stuff. There are many fantastic books by people far more insightful than me that cover the spiritual aspects of being a worship musician. That said, please know that I'm keenly aware of—and profoundly grateful for—the incredible price Christ paid on my behalf to express His love toward me, as well as the rest of mankind. Everything I do as a musician and otherwise is simply in response to this extravagant outpouring (see the "Coda" section for more of my thoughts on this).

I'd like to take a moment to express my heartfelt thanks to the many people who made this book possible. At the top of the list are Gina, Carly, and Lauren for love, support, and patience through the countless hours involved with this project. I'm so grateful for each of you! Big gratitude to Lincoln Brewster for the foreword; I'm thankful for our many years of playing, ministry, and friendship. Thanks to John Patitucci, Dominique Di Piazza, Michael Tobias, Bob Gallien, Bill Bartolini, and Steve Rabe for sharing your brilliant insights with us. Thanks, Steve Batz and Tim Devlin, for your artistry and generosity. Thanks to Bill Gibson, John Cerullo, and all at Hal Leonard for making me sound like I know what I'm doing! To Bruce and Judy Adolph, Matt Kees, and all at Christian Musician, thanks for your ongoing support and friendship, and for getting this whole idea of writing a book off the ground. The following have contributed to this endeavor in ways both small and huge: all in the Stockton, Sainz, and Gallo families; Roy and Chris Cochran and family; Keith and Mary Felch; David Owens; Rob Rinderer; Jeff Huntington; Mike Sessler; Ryan and Mindy Daffron and family; Mike Overlin; Doug Gould; Corey Fournier; Todd and Darla Gorton; Frank Reina; Joel Whitley; Suzie Stablein; Mark, Ali, and Daniel Cullen; Ken Baugh and all at Coast Hills; Monty Kelso; Holland Davis; Paul Baloche; Nalu's Island Grill; and every one of you ArtOfGroove.com subscribers. And thank You, Jesus, for *way* too much to list here!

In my haste, I inevitably forgot some names in the aforementioned list; I'm so sorry if it's you!

Anyway, thanks again for taking this time to invest in your playing; without further ado, plug in your bass, grab that espresso, and let's awaken the art of groove.

P.S. Much of the material is relevant to bass playing in any context, so if you're joining me and you're not a worship musician, welcome! I'm elated to have you aboard and hope you find this book helpful in your musical endeavors.

1

A Passion for the Groove

The most fitting starting point for this exploration of bass playing in a rhythm section is a discussion of the ensemble bass player's *raison d'etre* (reason for being). This might be familiar to many players, but even experienced bassists can benefit from revisiting these critical foundational concepts.

The bass guitar is a *rhythm*-section instrument. Its primary function, together with the drum kit, is to create a solid rhythmic foundation. In a nutshell, it's the bassist's job to *groove*. I define *groove* as a rhythmic feeling of consistent, predictable, and reliable forward motion in the music. The bass and drums fundamentally establish the groove and are essential to creating that feeling of consistent and reliable forward motion anytime they're playing. The other musicians depend upon that solidity and consistency. The parable of the two builders in Matthew 7—one who built his house on rock, the other on sand—and its parallels to music come to mind. The rhythm section is responsible for establishing that foundation upon which the musical house is built and ensuring that come rain, floodwaters, wind, or bad monitor mixes, everything will remain intact! So what does this all mean to the bass player?

As much as we might enjoy practicing warp-speed slap licks, contrapuntal tapping, harmonics, or otherworldly chord forms, those things are truly optional. I have yet to receive a call to play in a musical situation based upon any of the aforementioned and would venture to guess that neither have you. That's just not what most ensembles, particularly worship bands, are looking for from a bass player.

A player could conceivably play just the root notes of the chords—with unwavering, consistent groove and great feel—and perfectly fulfill the bassist's role. Everything else is really just frosting on the cake.

Now before you sell off your basses to pursue a flashier instrument, please stay with me a minute longer to hear my point! I have nothing against flashy bass playing. I enjoy bass pyrotechnics as much as the next bassist, and my CD collection has a healthy representation from the "bass in your face" contingent.

All of the preceding is simply to say: if you don't already have it, I want to encourage you to develop and nurture a *passion for the groove*. Getting right in there with the drummer and locking down a really solid and great feel is the most fulfilling musical experience a bassist can have, and that is the primary thing that other musicians pursue in a bass player. If you're unconvinced of this, please take a moment to track down a few of the busier bass players around your hometown. They will undoubtedly cite the ability to groove as the biggest musical factor keeping their phones ringing.

Personally, this passion for the groove required quite an adjustment from me as a musician. I had pretty much learned to play bass by emulating several prominent riff-oriented bassists. They were all wonderful musicians, but the *lead bass* style really only works well in those particular musical groups or similar ensembles where the arrangements and songwriting are tailored to accommodate that sort of playing. Unfortunately, in most other musical contexts, that approach to bass is inappropriate and obtrusive.

I had to refine my concept of the bassist's function from one of competing with the guitarist for sonic space and notes per bar to one of scaling back, doing everything in my power to make the song *feel* fantastic and giving the other musicians a sense of confidence and solidity.

That is the challenging and exhilarating higher calling that awaits the groove-oriented bassist! If you've never tried it, you have no idea what you're missing.

It's the best!

2

Fingerboard Familiarity

Keeping your focus on grooving is difficult when the fingerboard is a nebulous zone of uncertainty and trepidation! A solid understanding of how the notes are organized is essential for getting to the point where the bass is like an expressive paintbrush in your hands—instead of an obstacle to negotiate.

Memorizing the "Groove Range"

It's critical to memorize the names of the notes at the seventh fret and below (the *groove range* or area of the fingerboard where most groove playing occurs). There are a number of inherent characteristics of a bass tuned in standard, straight-fourths tuning (EADG) that will assist in this task.

Begin with the C major scale, which you probably already know is: C, D, E, F, G, A, B, C (see Figure 2-1, with suggested scale pattern or form on the fretboard).

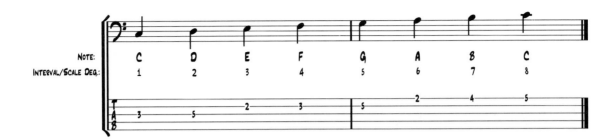

Figure 2-1. C major scale.

Octave Shape 1

Notice that the lowest and highest notes are both C, but they're one octave apart. Memorize the fretboard shape or relationship between these two notes. I refer to this commonly played pattern as "Octave Shape 1" ("My Sharona," anyone?). Using this shape in conjunction with each note of the C major scale, many more notes can be easily identified (see Figure 2-2).

Figure 2-2. Octave Shape 1 practice.

Note that the octave shape can be applied downward or upward, as apparent when playing the E (on the second fret of the D string) and the octave below (open E string).

Octave Shape 2

Notice that the second fret of the G string is an A, one octave above the A located at the fifth fret of the E string. I refer to this as "Octave Shape 2." This is not a particularly comfortable fingering to play, but it is invaluable in helping to tie the whole fingerboard together. In Figure 2-3, play the high notes on the G string and the lower notes on the E string. Try to memorize this shape to the point that you can play random notes on the G string and find the corresponding octave notes below on the E string. Then reverse the exercise, playing notes on the E string and their octaves above on the G string.

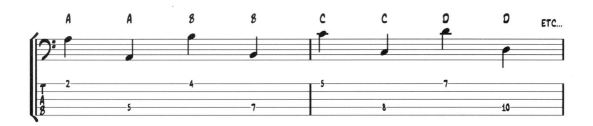

Figure 2-3. Octave Shape 2 practice.

The Fifth-Fret Rule

Here is one of the few things I retained from taking a couple of guitar lessons as an eight-year-old kid! The fifth fret of the E string is an A, and that's the same note as the open A string. Carry that logic through to the other strings: the fifth fret of the A string is the same as the open D string, the fifth fret of the D string is the same as the open G string, and so on. So no matter what string you're on, the fifth fret of that string is the same note as the next higher (smaller) string.

The Seventh-Fret Rule

The seventh fret of the A string is an E, one octave above the open E string. Similarly, the seventh fret of the D string is an A, one octave above the open A string, and so on.

Practice finding all occurrences of random notes (for example, all of the Fs, B♭s, C♯s, and so on) at the seventh fret and below. The goal is to reinforce this to the extent that it requires little to no thought. I've found this can only be accomplished through repetition— preferably on a daily basis. It's one of the critical "eating your veggies" aspects of learning to be an effective bassist. The good news is that it can be assimilated relatively quickly with consistent and diligent effort.

The fun stuff is on its way, but thriving as a worship bassist is utterly dependent upon a solid grasp of this foundational knowledge. Have you counted the cost? Are you committed to investing in the talents God's given you? Are you ready to take your musicianship to the next level? This is where it begins. Memorize that fingerboard!

The Intervals

In most contemporary-music environments, it would be unusual to hear players saying things like, "And when we get to that unison line, we all need to play do-re-mi. . . ." Instead, most modern music uses a numeric system based on *intervals*, which describe and define the difference in pitch between two notes. Memorizing the intervals is one of the most important things that can be done to develop fluency on the instrument, as well as an ability to verbally convey musical ideas to others. Many of you might already be familiar with intervals, but let's take a moment to ensure that we're all on the same page.

As I mentioned previously, the C major scale is: C, D, E, F, G, A, B, C. In terms of intervals, we refer to the scale numerically as 1, 2, 3, 4, 5, 6, 7, 8 (octave). In other words, D is the second relative to C, E is the third relative to C, and so on. For purposes of initially memorizing these intervals, please adhere rigidly to the scale pattern specified in Figure 2-1 of the "Memorizing the 'Groove Range'" section:

- C and D played on the A string.
- E, F, and G played on the D string.
- A, B, and C played on the G string.

Let's go back to that C major scale again. Play the C (third fret, A string), then the G (fifth fret, D string). As you can see, that would be the first and the fifth, respectively, in the key of C. Take a good look at the relationship between those notes, and memorize it. I refer to that shape as the *fifth above*—in a moment, you'll see why I clarify *above* versus *below*.

It's quickly apparent that on our wonderfully consistent and logically tuned instruments—guitarists may now turn green with envy—that shape can be transposed anywhere on the fingerboard. No matter what the lower note is, the higher note will always be the fifth above. This is an important point, because those interval shapes are not bound exclusively to the C major scale. If you transpose the aforementioned shape of the fifth above to the key of A (play the A at the fifth fret of the E string), you'll find that E (seventh fret, A string) is the fifth above, relative to A.

Go through the C major scale and memorize the shape of the second above, third above, and so on, all the way through the seventh above. Transpose each of those shapes all over the fingerboard to help reinforce them in any and all keys.

Once comfortable with those intervals, do the same thing for the intervals in the octave *below*. To assist with finding those shapes initially, I recommend thinking of the root as the eighth—or high-octave note—of Octave Shape 1.

Again, let's look at that C major scale. Relative to the high C (fifth fret, G string), the B (fourth fret, G string) is the seventh of the octave below, or more simply, the *seventh below*. Memorize that shape (a half step, with the higher note being the root) as the seventh below. Proceed by memorizing the remaining interval shapes for the octave below.

Here's a drill to help in the memorization of these intervals: Have someone call out random intervals ("third above," "fifth below," "seventh above," and so on), and think of each new note as the root note for the next interval. For instance, once the third above is played in the example, don't consider it to be the third any longer; rather, think of it as the root from which the fifth below is found. This exercise helps keep the focus on the interval shape exclusively without regard to a particular key. If you get stuck (e.g., someone asks for the seventh above when you're already on your highest string), just use Octave Shape 1 or 2 to buy some room on the fingerboard, and continue.

Once those intervals are assimilated, it's time to fill in the blanks by memorizing the sharps and flats. These would commonly be notated in music as ♯s and ♭s, respectively. G♭ is one fret lower than a G, right? Since G is the fifth relative to C, G♭ must be the flatted-fifth—or flat-fifth, flat-five, or ♭5; they're all synonymous terms. Memorize the shapes of the ♭3, ♭7, and so on, in the positions both in the octave above and below.

Three Essential Scales

Let's focus on several scales that I feel are essential for bassists in most contemporary music. This is by no means a comprehensive list and doesn't include many of the modes that are so important for navigating diatonic harmony (please refer to the "Suggested Resources" section for further information). However, these are bare-bones minimum, must-know scales.

Previously in this chapter, I discussed the C major scale. It's been included again (Figure 2-4), with suggested scale form.

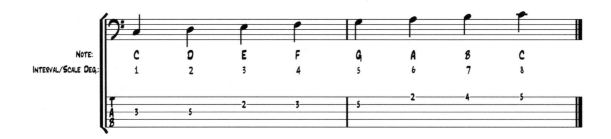

Figure 2-4. C major scale.

To apply some knowledge from last time, this scale is defined by the intervals: 1-2-3-4-5-6-7-8 (octave). The major scale is obviously a fundamental one to know and one with which all players should be comfortable. Generally speaking, it can be played over any major chord. I am quick to place a condition on that statement due to the modes. Based upon the function of a particular major chord relative to the key of a song, the proper scale may not be the major scale. A solid understanding of the modes allows a player to immediately know the appropriate scale to play.

The next essential scale is the natural minor. For purposes of comparison, the C natural minor scale is included with suggested pattern (Figure 2-5).

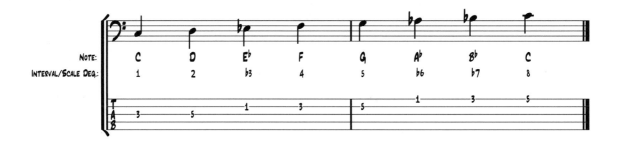

Figure 2-5. C natural minor scale.

It is defined by the intervals: 1-2- ♭3-4-5- ♭6- ♭7-8 (octave). You might be familiar with a fingering of this scale that doesn't require as much of a stretch; however, I feel that it's critical to learn this specific form, as it allows one to easily compare the relative differences and unique characteristics between the various scales one encounters. Based upon the scale pattern suggested, it is very clear that the third, sixth, and seventh scale degrees are flatted, with the remaining intervals being common to both the major and natural minor scales.

The last scale to cover is the Mixolydian mode. *Mode?* Yes, you're reading it correctly. This *is* one of the modes—as a matter of fact, so are the other two scales I just covered—but let's defer that detailed discussion to the "Suggested Resources." The Mixolydian mode (Figure 2-6) is defined by the intervals: 1-2-3-4-5-6- ♭7-8 (octave).

Figure 2-6. C Mixolydian mode.

Generally speaking—remember that phrase?—it can be played over a dominant seventh chord (C7, A7, etc.).

Once familiar with these scales in the key of C, transpose them up and down the fingerboard and get them under your fingers in the other keys as well.

Staggered Intervals

An excellent way to practice scales is to play them in staggered intervals. This involves playing through each degree of the scale followed by that note's relative third, fourth, fifth, or whatever interval you select.

To illustrate, try playing the C major scale in staggered thirds (Figure 2-7).

Figure 2-7. C major scale in staggered thirds (ascending).

Starting on the C or root note, the sequence would be: 1-3, 2-4, 3-5, 4-6, 5-7, 6-8, 7-9, 8. Do you see how that works? Each degree of the scale is the first note of a pairing, with the second note being the appropriate relative interval.

Now complete that exercise by playing the descending version (Figure 2-8): 8-6, 7-5, 6-4, 5-3, 4-2, 3-1, 2-7 (below), 1.

Figure 2-8. C major scale in staggered thirds (descending).

Use this method to play through the natural minor scale and Mixolydian mode as well. Experiment with staggered fourths, fifths, sixths, and sevenths. Your assimilation of these scales should improve dramatically, as the intervallic jumps—especially the wider ones such as sixths and sevenths—are rather unforgiving of guesswork!

I hope that this time spent focusing on the fingerboard has increased your understanding of the bass and your confidence as a result. As I move on to cover other topics, I encourage you to keep reinforcing these exercises; they are absolutely foundational to your playing.

3

The Spice

There are innumerable ways that the same intended message can be conveyed—with greatly varying degrees of effectiveness!

Suppose it's my wedding anniversary and I'd like to express my heart to my wonderful wife. I could (a) keep my eyes glued to the football game on the widescreen while managing to mumble, "Uh, I love ya"—between plays, of course—or (b) whisk her away to a candlelight dinner followed by a walk to the very spot where I proposed to her and whisper in her ear, "I love you."

Okay—enough mushy stuff! The obvious point is that the message in both of the above scenarios was the same, but it probably wasn't communicated as effectively in the first example. So what does this have to do with music? I'm so glad you asked!

The same piece of music can be played in a manner akin to my first example—devoid of any discernible emotion—or it can be played in a way in which listeners find themselves literally moved to tears. Effective musicians have the ability to truly communicate and convey passion on their instruments. Instead of listeners relating your playing to a telegram stating: "To whom it may concern: *Bass line. Bass line. Bass riff. Bass line . . .*" they find themselves profoundly impacted by the emotive musical statement being made.

There are countless elements involved in effectively communicating instrumentally; some of them are quite esoteric, while others are practical, technical matters. I'd like to explore the latter, to which I refer as "the spice."

That term refers to a number of different techniques that serve the same function, musically, as spices do in a culinary context. The discriminating use of spice in a particular dish is often what takes it from being bland and uninspired to really grabbing your attention—and communicating.

What are some of the different musical spices? The major ones would include phrasing techniques such as vibrato, slurs/hammers, dynamics, ghosting, note duration, register, and various rhythmic devices.

Dynamics

This is the simplest of all the spices to incorporate. Fundamentally, it simply involves playing certain things louder or with greater intensity while playing other things more quietly or with lesser intensity. Ironically, it is also perhaps the most often overlooked, despite the enormous effect it can have on the music.

To acquaint ourselves with the power of dynamics, we need only to listen to the difference between a parent's loving whisper of her toddler's name at bedtime and that same parent's anguished shriek of that child's name in a dire emergency. Same spoken word—but man, it's conveying two *entirely* different sentiments.

Musically, if you bulldoze your way through a set of tunes at full-throttle, *I'm-gonna-rip-the-frets-out-of-this-fingerboard* intensity, it will lose most of its impact by the second song. How long can we listen to people screaming at the top of their lungs before it just starts sounding like loud talking? However, contrasting dynamics, even relatively minor dynamic differences, can make that part of the tune where you and your bandmates "turn it up to 11" really have the desired effect.

In the same way that other forms of art or communication have ebb and flow—moments of pandemonium and car crashes interspersed between periods of quiet introspection and beautiful sunsets—music is generally enhanced with such diversity in dynamics.

A classic musician joke involves the exasperated drummer declaring his frustration with the bandleader as he screams, "What do you *mean* 'play with dynamics'? I'm playing *as loud* as I can!" I suspect that his quiet introspection and beautiful sunsets sounded a lot like his pandemonium and car crashes.

Over the next few months when practicing, make a deliberate and concerted effort to focus upon dynamics as you play through familiar tunes. A great place to start is to play the verse, chorus, and bridge sections of the tune, approaching each section with its own dynamic level. For instance, play the verse at a lower intensity and spend the last two or four bars gradually building up to a dynamically heavy chorus. Then as the chorus leads back into the next verse section, bring the dynamic level back down.

For these purposes, I encourage you to even go so far as to *exaggerate* the difference in dynamic levels between the sections. Listen intently—do you hear how the music seems to say more than when the dynamics are static?

If it's difficult for you to hear everything in context while you're actually playing, try recording yourself and listening back. Also, be aware that many musicians have a natural tendency to rush the tempo when increasing the dynamic and drag the tempo when playing softly. We'll tackle this in detail later. For now, concentrate on keeping the tempo consistent regardless of the dynamic level.

Once you're comfortable with this exercise, try to apply those enhanced dynamics to the tunes in your next band rehearsal. Again, in actual playing situations, dynamic variations can be subtle and still have a significant effect on the overall musical statement. You'll likely find that the old and familiar arrangements sound fresh and different as the other players respond—intentionally or otherwise—to the dynamic contrast in your playing.

Ghosting

Ghosting, or the playing of ghost notes, is a technique that involves playing muted, rhythmic "thuds" between the notes that are actually being voiced or fretted. They allow the player to relay additional rhythmic information to the listener and other members of the band. It is an incredibly useful means of conveying to our drummers exactly how we are subdividing and feeling the groove—while minimizing the sense that there's a massive and dense cluster of bass notes coming at them.

If you're unfamiliar with this technique, simply pluck notes as normal with your right or plucking hand, while lightly resting your left- or fretting-hand fingers on the strings. When the hands are executing this technique properly, the resulting sound will be rhythmic, having no discernible pitch.

This technique can be developed by playing one voiced or fretted note followed by one ghost note (Figure 3-1).

Figure 3-1. Ghost-note practice.

You will soon develop a feel for the right amount of pressure to exert with your fretting hand. Practice this exercise with a metronome set at 100 beats per minute (bpm). Rhythmic accuracy is important when employing ghost notes, so strive for absolute consistency with the click. If you aren't already, begin getting comfortable tapping your foot on the quarter notes, as this will reinforce your internal sense of the pulse. Listen closely for *flams* (spots where the metronome's click and your playing aren't precisely together).

The next step is to practice scales using alternating ghost notes (Figure 3-2).

Figure 3-2. A major scale with ghost notes.

Your right-hand technique will be as if playing the scale in eighth notes—two per note. The left-hand technique is similar to Figure 3-1 and involves playing the first note as usual, then releasing downward pressure upon the string so that the plucked second note is muted. Employ the scale pattern prescribed in the "Memorizing the 'Groove Range'" section (just transposed to A).

Let's compare two versions of the same bass line to illustrate the effectiveness of ghosting. In Figure 3-3, a simple groove in Am7 employs no ghost notes and implies an eighth-note subdivision.

Figure 3-3. Groove without ghost notes.

Notice how the bass line itself is rather ambiguous regarding the underlying pulse and feel of the groove. The line reflected in Figure 3-4, on the other hand, incorporates ghost notes to imply a sixteenth-note feel that was not present in the first version.

Figure 3-4. Groove with ghost notes.

Isn't it interesting how that subtle change results in such a different feel? Work on employing ghost notes in your own grooves—where musically appropriate, obviously!—to convey a deeper sense of time and feel to the rest of the rhythm section.

Incidentally, substituting fretted notes with ghost notes is perhaps the most effective way to simplify and refine a groove that seems too busy or note heavy. Listen to some of Francis Rocco Prestia's work with Tower of Power for inspiration and further insight into the potential of this technique.

Slurs and Hammers

Another often-overlooked element of phrasing is the use of slurs and hammers. More than just tools to help convey musical ideas emotively, they can also be extremely effective for smoothing out an otherwise obtrusive embellishment or lick—which will directly impact the degree to which your bandmates appreciate said embellishment!

Let me briefly describe the techniques involved. A *slur* is accomplished by plucking a fretted note, then sliding the fretting finger to a different note while maintaining downward pressure and without plucking the string a second time. A *hammer*—also sometimes referred to as a hammer-on—is similar, except that the fretting finger remains on the initial note while another finger on the fretting hand hammers down on a higher fret on that string. It results in a clearly defined attack on the second note—as opposed to the slide associated with slurring. Let your ears and musical sensitivity guide your application of these phrasing techniques.

Let's check out two versions of the same lick. Figure 3-5 reflects the straight version with each note being plucked individually.

Figure 3-5. Lick without slurs or hammers.

Figure 3-6, on the other hand, includes a few slurs and hammers to smooth out the line.

Figure 3-6. Lick with slurs and hammers.

Notice how the second version sounds a bit more like it's being *sung* on the bass rather than simply played?

Great vocalists use slurs frequently to make lines sound more natural and less mechanical. We instrumentalists can learn volumes by exploring and emulating the phrasing of talented and emotive vocalists.

Note Duration

An amazingly effective way to enhance your playing and the degree to which it speaks is through the use of variations in note duration. Simply put, this involves letting certain notes ring or sustain while muting other notes so that they are virtually thuds that vanish immediately after being played.

You've probably heard the terms *legato* and *staccato* used to differentiate between these two types of phrasing. *Legato* describes music where the notes are long and smoothly flow into each other. Staccato, on the other hand, describes musical phrases that are choppy, where each individual note is distinct and separate from the next.

The good news is that, next to dynamics, note duration is perhaps the most easily incorporated of the spices I've been discussing in this chapter. But the dividends in expressiveness are enormous!

There's nothing too challenging in getting notes to ring; simply keep downward pressure with your fretting finger on the string you've just plucked, and keep your plucking hand from touching that string! Unless you're playing a Hofner Beatle bass, the note should sustain reasonably well. Nothing derogatory intended about Hofners, by the way—I *love* the way they sound—they just aren't known for exceptional sustain.

To shorten the note duration, release downward pressure by your fretting finger after the string is plucked. Don't take your fretting finger off the string, though; leave it resting lightly there to mute. In addition to that fretting-hand technique, it is also very effective to simultaneously place a fingertip from the plucking hand—usually the other of the two plucking fingers normally alternating—onto that string when it should be muted. A bit of practice will make this a smooth motion that requires no significant effort or thought to execute.

Playing in a legato manner is surprisingly difficult to execute cleanly. Practice playing a bass line that uses quarter notes at a slow to moderate tempo. Concentrate on letting each note ring for its full value. That should result in notes that ring all the way up to each successive note, but with no overlap and no discernible rest between them.

For staccato playing, take that same bass line and try to mute each note immediately after it is played. Ensure that no other extraneous noises—clicks, ringing open strings, and so on—are evident between notes.

After that's comfortable, take it to the next level. Play a steady stream of eighth notes—preferably all the same fretted note, to eliminate variables and allow you to focus on note duration exclusively—along with a metronome set to quarter notes at 90 bpm, and play through the following variations.

- Version 1: Make each note staccato ("dut-dut-dut-dut . . .").
- Version 2: Let the first note be staccato, followed by a legato note
- ("dut-*duh*-dut-*duh* . . .").
- Version 3: The opposite of No. 2 above: play the first note legato, followed by a staccato note on the upbeat ("*duh*-dut-*duh*-dut . . .").

Work through the songs you typically play, and try to incorporate variations in note duration. I think you'll find it has a dramatic effect on the overall band performance of the tune. If you're phrasing a driving eighth-note line in a very ringy, washy manner, your drummer will invariably open the hi-hat just a bit more to give the groove a tad more "oomph." Conversely, if you tighten up that same line and phrase it in a really staccato manner, you'll find that the drummer—provided listening skills are employed!—will close the hi-hat and tighten up the overall feel. The other instrumentalists respond to these differences in feel, whether or not they are consciously aware of them.

Experiment with utilizing this concept for transitions between different sections of the tune. For instance, if the verse builds into the chorus, it is very effective to use the last bar or two of the verse to progressively let the notes ring out more and create a sense of escalating into the chorus. When bringing the tune back down after the chorus, tighten up the bass line once again.

Variations in dynamics work fabulously with this idea. Try to let those transitions coincide with similar peaks and valleys dynamically.

Now we're talking!

Vibrato

The use of vibrato is a big factor in making our instruments emote. Take the example of singers: if they never utilized vibrato, they would probably sound relatively bland, musically lifeless, or at least lethargic. The same phenomenon applies to instrumentalists. Appropriately placed vibrato is a very effective device to help a vocalist or instrumentalist communicate to an even greater extent.

As you're probably aware, vibrato is generally a slight modulation in pitch that gives a note a singing quality. It is usually applied to a note with a duration of two beats or longer, but context and song tempo—as well as the subjective area of taste!—may dictate otherwise.

The technique can be accomplished in a number of different ways. There's what I refer to as a "side-to-side" vibrato, which is accomplished simply by slightly rolling the fretting finger alternately toward the headstock and the bridge of the bass. The actual range of fretting-hand motion for the type of vibrato I'm describing is no more than an inch or so. It tends to be more of an acoustic-guitar type of technique, although some bassists find it effective. I don't use it very much except when playing the fretless bass; in that context, it really shines and helps produce the coveted fretless growl. For fretted basses, it can be a bit subtle for my taste. Nevertheless, it is one of several possible vibrato techniques.

One that I tend to use more often is the "up-and-down" version, which allows me to cover the range from subtle to overt with minimal effort. The basic fretting-hand position is similar to that of the aforementioned side-to-side method, but the motion of the fretting finger essentially alternates between pulling the fretted string toward the floor and pushing it toward the ceiling. For me, however, this version is most easily accomplished by keeping the fretting finger stationary and instead letting the up-and-down motion come from the forearm—versus isolated to the fretting finger alone. I encourage you to experiment and determine which is most comfortable for you.

It's quickly apparent that one can easily get aggressive with this form of vibrato. Aggressiveness is great at times, but might result in the fretted string being pulled completely off of the fingerboard—especially if the vibrato is being applied to a note on the G string—which could prove counterproductive if occurring in the middle of a ballad!

A third variation of the vibrato technique is what I call "the Abe"—after renowned bassist Abraham Laboriel Sr. He didn't invent this technique, but I feel that his style of funk bass playing really defined this type of vibrato. One can hear examples of it all over in his playing, and he uses it to great effect.

It's basically a side-to-side vibrato on steroids—a bit more radical and actually crossing over the frets. Where the side-to-side vibrato has a typical range of motion of approximately 1 inch, this method generally increases that range to approximately 2 to 3 inches. It involves a comparatively lighter touch, and the fretting-hand thumb acts as a pivot point. Incidentally, the fret buzz associated with this type of vibrato is actually desirable; it tends to give it that funkier tone.

In terms of context, the Abe is probably the least subtle of the vibrato techniques and something you'll most likely want to use sparingly. When appropriately placed, though, it speaks volumes!

The next time you're practicing through your band's material, try to find points where your bass line is fairly legato and might lend itself to some subtle vibrato. Although it's effective on low notes as well, you might find it even more so in the higher registers—especially those favorite bass-player licks involving slides up to the ninth!

Try to think of your phrasing in a manner similar to a vocalist. In much the same way that most great singers will hit and hold a note briefly before employing vibrato, instrumentalists can sound more relaxed and natural by easing into it. Vibrato will also lose some of its specialness if applied full-tilt to every note being played!

Experiment with the rate of vibrato too. You may find that a delicate and introspective ballad will benefit from a relatively slow rate, while an up-tempo fusion tune might be more conducive to a faster rate. Again, the best indicator for this is likely to be whether or not you can picture a vocalist singing the part as you're playing it.

I've covered a number of techniques that help make playing more communicative. I encourage you to use these different spices to take your playing to the next level of artistic expression.

My challenge to each of you is to approach your music from this day forward with a commitment to making your bass musically convey what the song is conveying lyrically and spiritually. If the lyrical message is jubilant, apply the "spice"—dynamics, phrasing, ghosting, and so on—to your bass line to make listeners want to jump to their feet and celebrate at the top of their lungs. If the song is expressing anguish, make your bass line drive them to tears. I'm really not advocating emotional manipulation, by the way. Rather, I'm simply encouraging you to ensure that the music and singing are consistent in what they're expressing.

Let's Grab Coffee: Sitting In

As bassists, we're generally functioning as support musicians. Unlike our ivory-tickling and guitar-twanging colleagues, we usually don't find ourselves leading our own bands or doing a great number of solo dates. Instead—and much to my preference, I might add—we often find ourselves being asked to sit in on a variety of different musical contexts.

In each of those diverse situations, though, our objective is invariably the same: give the music a great feel, let the other musicians feel like they've been playing with us for years, and—ideally—let them feel so comfortable with our support that they scarcely give a thought to the fact that their usual bassist couldn't make it! In other words, it is to lock in and groove.

Perhaps my favorite aspect of being a freelance bassist is the wonderfully broad range of musical contexts in which I find myself playing. From a purely musical perspective, I find it incredibly stimulating to go from playing in a modern worship setting on Sunday morning, to playing jazz fusion a few nights later, to subbing for a bassist in a heavy rock band a week later, to reading through hymns in a traditional service a few days after that.

Even if you're not a vocational musician, I urge you to pursue various playing situations as your schedule permits. You'll gain invaluable experience and get the exhilaration of s-t-r-e-t-c-h-i-n-g beyond your comfort zone!

Here are a few of the factors I've found to be important in having a successful experience sitting in.

Be Ye Prepared

- Arrive on time.
- Know the material in advance, if possible.
- Bring a pencil to scribble down notes on song form or arrangement that come up during rehearsal or soundcheck.
- Ensure that your gear is in good working order—with extra strings, 9V batteries, an AC power strip, and so on.

The Ministry of Groove

- Make sure you're *locking* with the drums—playing cohesively and functioning as a rhythmic unit with them. This is probably the single most important musical factor of all; this point cannot be overemphasized.
- Avoid "riffing-out," but rather play in a reserved manner, finding one or two places to inject subtle, tasteful, and musically appropriate fills.
- Play with dynamics.
- Play a part: those of us noodlers out there know who we are!
- Employ diversity in note duration and look for spots to leave rests.
- Avoid playing unnecessarily busy lines; let the part fit the song.
- Avoid blowing out the venue with your amp volume—even if it sounds good where you're standing. It's always preferable to be asked to turn up rather than turn down!

The Homework

- Read music: it opens up a whole world of other opportunities. It requires nothing more than repetition; practice truly makes perfect. I taught myself to read after I'd been playing for over 12 years; if I can do it, anybody can!
- Have a vocabulary in a number of different styles of music from which to freely draw. Develop the ability to be a musical chameleon; make it sound and feel like your favorite style of music is that of the current tune.

Light and Salt

- Have a great attitude! Be easygoing. Don't stress out.
- Smile!
- Be gracious and express genuine gratitude for the invitation to play.
- Be complimentary when you like what you're hearing from the other musicians; it blesses them, but also confirms that you're *listening.*
- In a word: *Koinonia*—fellowship and communion with other believers, if applicable—don't approach it as "just a gig."
- In cases where pay or an honorarium is involved, avoid being money oriented. If necessary, bring it up in a very easygoing manner on your way out the door or contact them the following day.

Go for it!

If you've hesitated to take that step beyond your normal musical situation, I wholeheartedly encourage you to be open to what the Lord brings along. You'll be amazed at the musical growth that can be realized through this type of experience. Additionally, it's a fantastic exercise of your faith to venture into that unexplored territory. Have a blast!

4

Tools of the Trade

Let's take a short break from groove concepts and bass line approaches—topics that can be elusive and difficult to quantify—and proceed onward to a subject that is more easily grasped and always close to a bassist's heart: *gear*!

Bass Factors

Many volumes have been written on the topic of selecting an electric bass guitar, and this is not intended to be an all-inclusive analysis. These are simply some of the primary considerations for me; I hope this information proves helpful for you as well.

Surviving "Option Anxiety"

I could spend many years discussing all of the variations and options to consider when selecting a bass. They come in every conceivable configuration. A quick stroll through your favorite music store should convince you of this fact. A bassist is faced with choosing between:

- Electric solidbody versus acoustic versus semi-acoustic.
- Bolt-on versus neck-through versus glue-in neck.
- A myriad of wood choices—or graphite or other man-made material—for neck, fingerboard, and body, or any combination thereof.
- Fretted versus fretless—or *fanned frets*, if you want to see something truly unique.
- Passive versus active electronics.
- Flatwound strings versus roundwound versus groundwound versus halfround (sounds a bit like I'm talking about cuts of beef!)

A term I've heard attributed to the legendary guitarist Pat Metheny is very applicable: *option anxiety*.

Prior to journeying down the road of assessment of the above considerations, I'd like to share a couple of thoughts and conclusions I've reached from many years of bass-related purchases.

First and foremost, I must reiterate what many of the top musicians frequently express: to a huge degree, *the tone is in the hands*. That is to say, if late bass legend Jaco Pastorius could walk into a music store today and play a dozen different basses, they would *all* have that "Jaco tone." Sure, there would be some differences based upon a particular instrument's construction, electronics, string type, and so on, but fundamentally, the most important factor contributing to the sound is the player. If you've been buying and selling Fender Jazz basses for decades in a seemingly futile effort to locate that perfectly beat-up, Jaco-esque early '60s model—so you can finally attain that *tone*—please take note. Jaco himself spoke of this as well.

I also firmly believe that there's no single instrument that does it all. Much as we all dream of heading to gigs with that solitary axe capable of everything we can imagine, we are simply kidding ourselves if we expect to get Marcus Miller slap tone, P-bass warm thuds, that almost hollow-ish acoustic-upright timbre, and growling electric-fretless *mwah* out of a single bass. Working bassists would be saving a ton of money on cartage and/or a ton of wear and tear on their backs if that were possible! Consequently, I recommend that players identify the instrument characteristics that are best suited for achieving the desired sound, or degree of playability and so on, and then find the particular instrument that best meets those criteria while staying within their budgetary constraints. Ideally, the instrument will also be capable of covering some of the other tonal needs, but it should definitely hit the primary targets.

I encourage you to listen to a multitude of different bassists and check out what type of gear is being used by the players whose sounds you like. Chances are that there are some shared features between their basses, even if there are different brand names. For example, decent slap tone can be achieved on basses from a broad range of manufacturers, but most basses capable of that tone share certain common traits: roundwound strings, fretted neck, and active electronics. One could painstakingly evaluate fretless acoustic bass guitars with tapewound strings and never come across a single one that delivered the Victor Wooten thumb tone. 'Nuff said!

Nine-String or Four-String...That Is the Question.

One of the fundamental decisions will be whether to go with the traditional four-string bass or to delve into the realm of extended range—whether five-string or beyond. Some incredible music is and has been made on four-string basses such as the legendary Fender Precision or Jazz, so one shouldn't base this decision upon any notion that such basses are somehow outdated. Instead, I would urge you to truly consider what you, specifically, seek to say on the instrument. If the very reason you decided to be a bassist—as opposed to a flautist—is an overwhelming affinity for sub-bass frequencies that pulsate from neighboring vehicles, then you might want to consider something with a low B string. If your stylistic preferences lean more toward classic rock or folk, then your best choice is probably the good ol' four. Bottom line: decide what you need, and resist the temptation to cart along extra strings that remain unused; they'll only contribute to muting difficulties.

Scale Length

The modern electric bass normally features a scale length (the distance between the nut and the bridge saddle) of 34 inches. Particularly since the onset of extended range basses, builders have found that a longer scale length—typically 35 inches, but sometimes even longer—generally enhances the tone and pitch clarity of the low B string. In general, I think a 35-inch scale is the way to go with a five- or six-string bass.

It should be mentioned that many brands of bass string don't readily accommodate this longer scale length because the silk wrap extends beyond the point on the string where it passes over the nut. Check into that beforehand, especially if you're inseparably attached to a certain brand or line of string!

Neck/Body Joint

The philosophy regarding the preferred method by which the neck is attached to the body has evolved considerably over the years. The original Fender basses featured necks that were bolted onto the body, and other manufacturers later utilized a glued neck-to-body joint. Gradually up through the '80s, the industry came to regard the neck-through design—where the neck extends the full length of the instrument and the body is essentially two "wings" that are glued onto opposite sides of the neck—as the most effective way to build a bass. Many of the high-end basses from that period feature this type of construction. The prevailing thought was that the neck-through design afforded the most stable neck with enhanced sustain.

The trend in recent years has largely veered back to the bolt-on design. Renowned luthier Michael Tobias believes this method results in a tone that's perceived to be clearer in the low frequencies—ironically, due to less fundamental in the sound. He explains that a neck-through generally contains more of the fundamental in the tone, which results in a perceived *lack* of clarity in the context of an actual mix. It *is* an intriguing concept. I can only say that as a player, I definitely concur that the perceived punch of my bolt-on basses well exceeds any neck-through bass I've owned or played, particularly for slapping or other percussive techniques. There are certainly differing opinions in the industry regarding this issue, but it is interesting to observe the proliferation of basses in the $3,000+ price range that feature bolt-on necks.

"Fret Not...It Only Leads to Evil" (Psalm 37:8)

Fretted or fretless: ideally, I don't think this should be an "either/or" proposition. Fretted bass and fretless bass are really two entirely different instruments in terms of tone and musical application. Sure, they both occupy the same register, are tuned in fourths, and so on, but they're such different colors in the sonic palette that I think it's truly valuable to have both at your disposal.

The fretless bass can be approached in much more of a hornlike manner when playing in an ensemble simply due to the timbre—that coveted "mwah factor"! At the same time, though, there are intonation considerations that generally necessitate much more attention than is usually needed when mowing through a tune with the trusty fretted counterpart. One useful feature is a lined fingerboard, which will give the player a general idea of the note location—but take note that fret lines do not guarantee accurate intonation. There is no substitute for big ears and consistent practice!

If you're not familiar with the sound of a fretless bass, some well-known examples are Nathan East's work on Eric Clapton's "Tears in Heaven" and Pino Palladino's playing on Paul Young's "Every Time You Go Away."

The Material World

Once you've solidified the decision on the essentials, it's time to consider the materials from which the bass is built.

In recent years, we've seen a number of synthetic materials—graphite necks, phenolic fingerboards, and so on—incorporated into bass construction. The overwhelming majority of basses, however, are still comprised of wood bodies, necks, and fingerboards. Due to space considerations, I'll limit my focus here to the characteristics of the most commonly used woods.

Luthier Michael Tobias again is a terrific source of information as he shares some of his vast insight into the tonal qualities of various woods. Michael is one of the premier bass builders in the world today, and is generally regarded as an authority in the field. I've condensed and formatted his comments below for ease of reference.

It should be prefaced that, according to Michael, the manner in which the various woods are combined—for example, poplar body, maple neck, wenge fingerboard—is critical to the overall tonal characteristics of the resulting instrument, and there are myriad combinations that can achieve similar results. Through years of experimentation, he's reached certain conclusions about which combinations fairly consistently attain certain qualities. He goes on to say that there are general rules about tonewoods, but that they're far from infallible.

Body

- **Alder:** "Big and warm."
- **Maple:** "Bright and clear."
- **Ash (Swamp):** "Hollow mids, punchy bottom."
- **Ash (Northern):** "Aggressive mids, punchy bottom."
- **Poplar:** "Punchier than northern ash, slightly less growl."
- **Mahogany:** "Round and pianolike, strong midrange."

Note on Laminated Tops: Michael expressed that a top with a thickness of 1/8 inch or less is generally cosmetic in nature with only a very slight effect on tone. He feels that the top will become more of a factor, tonally, at thicknesses of 5/16 inch or more.

Neck

- **Maple:** "Bright, with 'open' bottom."
- **Purple Heart:** "Similar to maple, but not as sweet."
- **Wenge:** "More focused and *slightly* compressed."

Laminated Necks: According to Michael, three-piece necks are purported to be more stable and less prone to dead spots. He was quick to point out that he's observed many contrary examples. Laminates are frequently done for cosmetic purposes or to save wood.

Fingerboard

- **Rosewood:** "Warmer, nice edge on top."
- **Ebony:** "Very clear, hard on top, 'clicky' for slapping."
- **Maple:** "Less fundamental, lows sound tighter."
- **Wenge:** "Characteristics between maple and ebony."

Strings

The type of string will profoundly impact the sound of the instrument for obvious reasons! A quick trip to the music store will likely reveal a multitude of options.

To simplify the matter, there are fundamentally two varieties: *roundwound* or *flatwound*. Without going into great detail, most strings consist of a wire core—round when viewed in cross section—with an additional wire wound around that core. When the latter also has a round cross section, the string is classified as roundwound. When the latter is a flat outer wrap when viewed in cross section, the string is classified as flatwound. Roundwound strings are known for their brightness, with a sparkly brilliance in the high end that is well suited for the slap technique or achieving any sort of tone with "bite." Flatwound strings are on the other end of the tonal spectrum and are known for a big, warm, sometimes thudlike timbre with minimal fret or finger noise. Some popular players known for the roundwound tone include Marcus Miller and Chris Squire, while wonderful examples of the flatwound sound can be heard on most of the classic Motown hits.

Once you've chosen the general type of string you'd like to use, you can experiment with different brands and the myriad of variations, different string gauges, and so on to achieve your own optimal balance of tone and playability. The biggest playability considerations are string tension and overall feel.

Onboard Electronics

One of the things I'm grateful for is that I don't have to be an expert in everything! I approach technology from the perspective of the player and know what works well for me, but I love being able to tap the vast expertise of experts in their respective fields.

Two such experts graciously agreed to sit down with me a while back and share their insight into the world of onboard electronics. It would be difficult to find two more qualified voices to speak to this topic, and it's truly remarkable that these giants of the industry remain so enthusiastic to share their knowledge and experience. A deep passion for the topic and genuine humility were clearly evident in each of them.

The topic of onboard electronics can be tricky; it's a vast and complex field where objective science meets subjective tone judgments. I felt it would be valuable to compile some insightful excerpts—those nuggets of wisdom I mentioned at the beginning of this book.

It is noteworthy that, even between recognized experts, there isn't complete consensus in some issues relative to onboard electronics; for instance, compare their slightly different views on the issue of onboard versus rack-mount systems.

So here are some thoughts from the experts. I hope you find their comments as provocative and informative as I did.

BILL BARTOLINI'S PERSPECTIVES

Bill Bartolini is the founder of Bartolini Pickups and Electronics, one of the world's premier manufacturers of bass pickups. He is highly respected as an authority in the field.

The Noise Factor

"Players tend to expect that one can put on huge amounts of treble boost without noise. The best hand-picked electronics out there will still introduce electronic hiss when you boost the treble—there's just no way around it. The "noiseless treble boost" does not exist. Bass? No problem. Mids? No problem—sweepable mids with a relatively narrow bandwidth are also okay as long as the bandwidth doesn't get too wide."

EQ Clarified: Shelving vs. Peak

"Usually tone controls are shelving bass, shelving treble, peak mids—sometimes one or two of these—with a sweepable or switchable frequency.

"Let me give a quick illustration of the difference between *shelving* and *peak* controls. Suppose you put on a treble boost and up to 500 Hz the response is flat. From 500 Hz, the response starts rising. It goes up x number of decibels, then it flattens out. And from say, 5 kHz or 6 kHz on out, it's relatively level. That's a shelf or plateau. If it was peaking, you might say that it starts at 500 Hz, peaks at 4 or 5 kHz, and then drops off on the other side, so that at 15 kHz, it is down."

Switchable vs. Sweepable

"My preference in midfrequency controls is that they should be switchable, because with sweepable—particularly if the range of sweep is big—there is a problem in performance. To go from one setting to another, you're hunting small motions of the knob that are translating into large changes in frequency—and you're doing this onstage, live. This doesn't work out very well. Switchable may seem a little restrictive sometimes—perhaps in a studio situation when you're hunting for that "just so" equalization—but in a live setting, it's more practical.

"We try to position our switching frequencies such that something helps fingerpicking—low-mid enhancement—something is in the middle range and is fully usable boost or cut, and something is around 800 Hz to 1 kHz and as a dip can give a good, depressed-mid slap tone. The shelving controls—bass and treble—can also be moved all over the place."

Onboard vs. Outboard Gear

"This was something on our minds when we designed a three-band system in the mid '90s. We wanted the lowest noise we could get—something that would compete with a rackmount unit. It's important to understand that rack units have the advantage in that the amount of electrical current available to them is far beyond what a battery can provide by many times. In designing a battery-powered system, you want to spare the battery a bit—you really don't want a battery to last less than a week. So we hunted for the best compromise between current draw and noise. Actually, I don't think it really ended up being much of a compromise at all—it doesn't need that much current—and I know that if I were to do a rackmount, I would use the same basic engine. I'm not going to claim that we've tested everything that's out there, but we've done a lot of testing. It's just a very nice engine."

Pickups and Placement

"This is crucial. The electronics can only modify the voicing that's already there. The voicing is going to be determined by the wood, the pickup, and the strings. The instrument itself is going to establish a voicing in terms of overall balance, peaks in the wood resonances, and so on. Besides that, the pickup is put in a particular spot. Besides *that*, your pickup can be narrow aperture—which defines what segment of the string the pickup is sensing, very accurately and perhaps with treble enhancement— or can be a very full tone and very good in the lows and sweet in the upper treble. There are a multitude of different possibilities in how the instrument can be voiced.

"There is a definite difference depending upon the aperture. If you're sensing the string with a narrow aperture like a single-coil, it's sensing that much of the *ripple* (the string motion is essentially a ripple which travels back and forth). With a dual-coil where the two coils are 1.5 inches apart—like a wide humbucker, for instance—it's sensing a wider "window" or aperture. Essentially, you cannot sense a ripple smaller than the window; the aperture limits your ability to sense treble. So if you have a 1.5-inch aperture, you're not sensing the upper treble nearly as well—or perhaps at all—compared to the lower frequencies. If you have a very narrow aperture—for example, single-coils, small pole pieces—then you are sensing the smallest ripple that you can."

Tone: Bass or Electronics?

"I am a believer that the tone really starts with the instrument's inherent acoustic characteristics. But at the same time, we use that. We have a test bass—one of many—in which we can exchange pickup systems in less than 5 seconds. This is critical, because in 10 seconds, some of the tone judgments go away. If you're looking at subtle things in the upper treble, the time that it takes to exchange pickups is close to where your tone memory goes away. Anyway, the test instruments are pretty neutral; they're not what you would be proud of as a luthier for resonance and tone— they are fairly dead. On the other hand, that is the challenge for the pickup. Unless the pickup really shines, it is not going to overpower that instrument's lack of resonance."

STEVE RABE'S PERSPECTIVES

Steve Rabe—or Steve W. Rabe—is the S. W. R. of amplification manufacturer SWR. His contributions to the world of bass amplification and electronics are huge. Subsequent to selling his ownership of SWR, he founded Raven Labs and proceeded to build electronics that many bass players consider indispensable.

Take a Load Off

"I believe that the main advantage of active electronics—especially as a buffer—is impedance matching. If the manufacturer or designer has missed the boat on that first thing, then everything else is a moot point in my opinion. The pickup naturally is a passive component, and it feeds, for instance, an amplifier. The amplifier's input impedance may or may not affect the true sound of your pickup. Suppose you're running out of a passive pickup, then into a tuner, then into an amp: that tuner may be loading down your instrument to a certain extent—it depends upon how well things are designed—but having an onboard preamp that is designed correctly will ensure that you're always going to get the same sound out of your instrument no matter what you plug into."

Evaluating Onboard Electronics

"As far as onboard equalization (EQ), that can vary a lot. I've heard some onboard EQ that was extremely noisy and colored the sound, where others have been done very well. So I'd recommend taking and listening to a bass or treble control and see if it just boosts or cuts the lows or highs—without adding too much hiss—or does it sound like it's clouding the sound? Really listen. Run the amp flat and see what the onboard electronics are doing by themselves. If you need your amplifier to alleviate problems caused by the onboard electronics, they might as well not be there. Rick Turner [*renowned luthier*] is a big proponent of having one knob on his instrument—volume—if that! Also, do the same thing with the volume knob: I've heard a lot of active instruments where the tone changes when the volume knob is halfway up—the highs are missing or the lows are missing or something like that. That's poorly designed onboard electronics."

"Guzinta–Guzouta"

"I believe that it's basically true; you can't put a $3,500 rack worth of sophisticated electronics into an instrument—maybe they'll be able to in the future with microchips. With onboard electronics, you run into more compromises in your design. Bear in mind, every design has its compromises—whether it's that $3,500 rack system or a $35 onboard system—so you have to listen for and try to recognize what compromises were taken in that design. That stated, if you had active electronics that were just a buffer—which I define as a *Guzinta–Guzouta* (everything that guzinta, you wanna guzouta)—and it did that very well, that would ensure that $3,500 piece of rack gear can do all that it is capable of doing."

Amplification

All of the aforementioned coolness doesn't do us much tangible good until we can amplify the signal! I'd like to once again emphasize that this isn't a comprehensive discussion of the topic but rather a summary of what I consider the primary factors.

The Basics

Before I start, let me quickly clarify a few terms.

- **Preamp:** Responsible for taking the signal from the instrument and, as the name suggests, providing minimal amplification in preparation for the earthshaking effects of the power amp. It usually affords a certain amount of equalization or tone shaping.
- **Power Amp:** Amplifies the signal to the extent that it can drive speaker cabinets.

Generally speaking, amplification is accomplished utilizing one of three formats:

- A self-contained unit that combines a preamp, power amp, and speaker cabinet—commonly referred to as a *combo amp.*
- A separate *amp head* consolidating the preamp and power amp.
- Separate components for each function—commonly referred to as a *rack system.*

Generally, the above sequence also tends to parallel the amount of expenditure necessary to acquire such a system. Combo amps are usually the least expensive—although a number of manufacturers now have high-end versions that sound quite good and can cost a small fortune—while having a consolidated amp head is probably the most prevalent among working bassists, due to the fact that it is arguably the best balance between performance, convenience, and portability. Then there are the audiophile ranks who have (or *had*) the big bucks and are only satisfied with individual components!

Let's All Say It Together: "Headroom"

For me—regardless of whether or not one's preferences lean toward a combo amp, amp head, or rack system—the single most important consideration is fairly simple: exactly how much power does the amp have? It all boils down to one word: *headroom.*

Have you ever noticed that most unbearably loud guitar amps are only rated at 100 watts? Yet, have you ever tried to get similarly deafening sound pressure levels from a 100-watt bass amp? You probably found that the closer you came to those high volume levels, the more your bass sounded like the aforementioned guitar amp—complete with an unusable amount of distortion. Without getting into the technical aspects, it is a fact that it requires far more power to reproduce low frequencies accurately than high frequencies. Additionally, the majority of musical contexts require a bass tone that is clean or undistorted without regard to volume. The latter dictates that the amplifier have enough power to be comfortably purring—as opposed to puffing, panting, and gasping just to keep up the pace—when turned up to the highest volume level at which you expect to play on a regular basis. Consequently, it is not uncommon to find bass amplifiers with power ratings in the range of 1,000 watts or higher. It's not for the purpose of turning up to 10 and testing the structural integrity of the venue's rafters, but rather to be able to attain your desired volume level without necessitating turning up any higher than to 40 to 50 percent of the system's maximum output. This extra margin or headroom also helps accommodate the *transients* (momentary spikes in volume) associated with some percussive techniques or playing dynamics without sending your tone into Fuzzville (no offense to residents of Fuzzville).

Impedance for the Rest of Us

An often-overlooked element when selecting an amplifier is impedance. Check to see what the power rating of the amplifier is when powering a load with impedance correlating with the cabinet(s) you intend to use. I'm not a technoid, but I did discover the practical significance of this factor when I acquired a couple of 8-ohm cabinets many years ago. While powering both cabinets reduced the load to 4 ohms—resulting in lots of output at fairly conservative volume settings on the amp—running just one cabinet necessitated that I run my 800-watt head in bridged-mono mode and fairly high volume settings just to drive the cabinet adequately. More on this in the "Speakers and Cabinets" section, by the way.

Tube Versus Solid State/Analog Versus Digital

There are many who are hardcore advocates of tubes, while others are just as adamant about the merits of solid-state circuitry. My personal views on this have evolved a bit over the years. I had long felt that tubes were less of an issue for bassists than they were for guitarists, where tube saturation is an essential element of the tone. Some of my colleagues at the time might have taken issue with that statement, as they murmured under their breaths about the unmatched warmth of tube tone, loaded their 150-pound all-tube heads into their cars, and dropped by their chiropractors on the way to the gig. But I digress. Through subsequent years of playing much more rock music, I came to appreciate that good bass tone in that context frequently involves a bit of dirt or saturation. Tubes, whether physical or emulated through the various circuits or software available today, can do wonderful and musical things to the sound of a bass.

A fantastic design trend has been to incorporate hybrid preamps—employing both tube and solid-state stages that can be blended to tonal preferences—with solid-state power amps into one head. This allows for the warmth of tubes to be introduced in the preamp stage while the virtues of high-power, solid-state circuitry can be realized for clean amplification.

The huge popularity of digital amplifiers in recent years adds to our choices. They have undeniably come a long way and sound quite good, primarily when taking into consideration the tremendous weight difference that generally exists between comparably rated analog and digital amps. Although there is a sound difference, when facing a choice between a heavy analog amp or a 3-pound digital amp that can be tossed into a gig bag, lots of gigging players conclude that the portability factor trumps any sonic differences.

Features

In addition to the above considerations, there are many features commonly found on amps these days. You'll want to assess your individual needs and seek out the gear with the features you require—at a price you can tolerate without hospitalization.

Here are some of the biggies for me:

- **Tone-Shaping/Equalization:** Graphic, parametric, or semiparametric.
- **Direct Output:** XLR output to send to the front-of-house PA system.
- **Pre- or Post-EQ Output:** Allows you to send the house either the flat signal directly from the bass or the signal with your EQ settings.
- **Tuner Output.**
- **Bypass Switch.**
- **Multiple Inputs:** Very convenient if using the amp for teaching.
- **Multiple Outputs:** Very convenient when a bandmate asks for an individual send from your rig.
- **Bi-Amp Mode:** Separate amplification for lows and highs (see Bob Gallien's interview in the next section for more on this).
- **Speakon Speaker Connectors:** Many of the high-end cabinets now utilize this improved type of connector.
- **Fan On/Off Switch:** Quite convenient to be able to silence the amplifier during recording.
- **Aux Send/Return:** For effects loop, and so on.

Speakers and Cabinets

As I mentioned earlier, I'm thankful to know experts in various fields so that I don't have to be one! I definitely know what I like and what works for me from a musical perspective, but when the discussion gets deeply into the science involved…let's just say that I am the furthest thing from a technoid.

I was honored and grateful to get some insight into the technical aspects of speakers and cabinets from none other than Bob Gallien, owner and founder of Gallien-Krueger (GK). GK has been at the forefront of bass amplifier and speaker design since the late '60s.

It was quickly apparent that any discussion of speaker and cabinet design involves a lot of physics and generally very heady stuff. Bob did a great job of simplifying where possible, but I've again excerpted the nuggets to give nontechies like me a reasonable chance of grasping the basic concepts without getting bogged down in the science. Should you have a burning desire to delve into the science involved, Bob suggests Wikipedia as a good resource: search under "loudspeaker" and "loudspeaker enclosure" to get started.

Speaker Sizes

"We build what the market wants—that's the simplest answer. Back in the day, we built 18s like everyone else. But the size of the speaker kind of follows the trends in music and what players are trying to get out of their equipment—and 18s over the years have just proven to be way too woofy. Players today seem to want a more articulate sound—they want to do more than just stand at the back of the stage and make a rumble.

"Horns can be useful for slap or really articulate types of playing, but for the growly rock tone that GK is known for, horns aren't necessary. What some manufacturers do, though, is put a horn in a cabinet to cover the top end, but if you turn off the horn, you notice that the woofers don't have any top end at all—nothing above 2 to 3 kHz. There's absolutely no growl.

"Our woofers are extended range—to 5 to 6 kHz—so you can get a nice, full-bodied sound without a horn. It's hard to do: it takes big magnets for high flux density, edgewound flat wire voice coils, expensive cone materials—you have to do everything you can.

"Again, it's really easy to tell the quality of the woofer in a cabinet—just turn off the horn: if the top end disappears and there is no flavor, you know.

"With the extended range that we get—in our 12, in particular—it's changed the whole meaning of a 12 from what it was years ago (or even with all the other brands that are out there now) because they go up really well in frequency, like a 10."

Cabinets

"You can make a decent, inexpensive cabinet if you make it out of particleboard—as many do, because it's dense and cheap. But particleboard weighs a ton and isn't very durable if it gets dropped or gets wet. If you want to build a *light* cabinet that sounds good, it's a lot tougher. You have to use a light material—we use a poplar variant of plywood which is light and strong. When you build with a plywood like that, you have to brace it a lot inside to make the cabinet stiff.

"If the side walls of a cabinet are flexible, energy goes out those side walls—and it's out of phase with what's coming out the front, which really knocks off the low-end response. So you want the side walls to be really stiff. That way, the energy is coming out of either the port or the speaker.

"Then comes the tuning. Tuning affects the way the cabinet resonates when you stop the note—kind of like when drummers put pillows or blankets inside their kick drum to make it sound more like a thud. Factors include the material—and how much of that material—you line the box with for damping, the stiffness of the box, the area of the port, the length of the port, the volume of the cabinet, and the resonant parameters of the speaker itself. It's very complicated, and that's where all the "black art" is in designing cabinets and speakers! Everybody has their own ideas of how to tune their cabinets, and the result is there are a lot of different-sounding cabinets on the market.

"Ports—when they're working—give a lot of extra "umph" to the lower end of the speaker. They can really screw up the sound of a speaker, too: they can make them boomy like a kick drum with no damping, or they can really tighten up the sound. There are all kinds of things that can happen, good or bad, with a port. So if you do it right—you know what you're trying to achieve and you achieve it—you can get some nice results with a port. But it's not necessarily always a good thing."

Neo vs. Ceramic

"The great thing about neodymium magnets is that they're incredibly lightweight. Up until the last few years, though, it's been difficult to get neo speakers to handle the power, due to overheating issues with the voice coils when you didn't have a heavy ceramic magnet. But we've figured out how to conduct the heat out of the voice coil and into the speaker frame so it can be radiated away—just about everybody's figured out how to do this—so neo speakers are now able to handle the kind of power that speakers with ceramic magnets do.

"In terms of the sound, neo magnet systems do have a different kind of sound than ceramic magnets. It gets kind of technical, having to do with ceramic magnetic circuits and something we call eddy currents that sort of fight what's happening with the voice coil. Those eddy currents are much lower in a neo system. So a neo speaker has a more linear sound than a ceramic speaker—it doesn't add as much color of its own."

Bi-amping

"We use a bi-amp solution because of this problem of growl. If you take that growly sound that comes from the power-amp structure and run it through a horn, it just doesn't work—it sounds like a buzz saw. So we separate our signal into a low-frequency portion and a high-frequency portion if you want to use a horn. At that point, the signals are still pretty clean. When the low-frequency portion goes through its power amp, it gets the growly sound and goes to the woofer by itself. The growly sound doesn't get put into the tweeter—which is powered by its own dedicated amp— so the tweeter stays clean.

"It's also nice to be able to control the level of the horn on the front panel of the amp instead of having to reach around to the back of the cabinet.

"Another reason for bi-amping is that we don't blow horns. In a non-bi-amped system, you've got a little horn that's rated at 50 watts and a 500-watt amplifier trying to pump energy into it. People blow those horn diaphragms all the time. But in a bi-amp system, there's a 50-watt amp—that's only putting 25 watts into that 8-ohm horn—so we don't lose those horns."

Impedance

"We make 4- and 8-ohm cabinets. I don't like 4-ohm cabinets. I don't like low-impedance cabinets in general. I don't like low-impedance speakers. It's more expensive to build a 500-watt amplifier that puts 500 watts into 8 ohms versus 2 ohms. If you're driving a low impedance like that to get your power, you're losing so much power in the speaker cord and you lose control of the cone. It's better to drive higher-impedance cabinets so that the 1/10th ohm impedance that's in your speaker cords and all your jacks and connectors is a lower contributor to the impedance of the total system—so you can still control the cones and have damping. I prefer 8-ohm cabinets, and we design our amplifiers to drive high impedances so you don't have those problems with the connector cords. If you're going to drive two 8-ohm cabinets to get 4 ohms, we use two cords from the amplifier—instead of daisy-chaining from one cabinet to the other. That gives you the best overall cone control.

"Cone control is critical at *high volume*, especially if you've got the growly thing going like we do. You've got to control those cones—otherwise it farts out. It boils down to high-impedance speakers, low-impedance speaker cables, good connectors, and a good amplifier with lots of current capability to drive it."

Near-Field vs. Far-Field

"Here's a quick physics lesson:

"Air is a low-impedance medium for sound to travel in. A sound wave has two components: pressure and velocity. A speaker is high-impedance—it delivers high-pressure/low-velocity waves—so when a sound wave leaves a speaker, it's really not matching the impedance of the air. As a wave propagates into a medium where there's a mismatch in the impedance, like air, it takes a few wavelengths for it to develop properly into the impedance, and eventually it will become a low-pressure/high-velocity wave. That takes 3 to 4 wavelengths, which is about 30 to 40 feet for a 100-Hz low-frequency sound wave.

"Your ear is designed to intercept waves that are low pressure/high velocity, so it hears much better as you get further away from the speaker. That's why 810s got so popular in the '80s. All that speaker area can launch a lower-pressure/higher-velocity wave right near the cabinet, so the player on the stage hears a more fully developed sound that's more closely matched to what the ear is designed to hear. But an 810 is a lot to lug around!

"For up-close listening, you're generally going to get a more accurate representation of your sound the more speaker area you have. Let's compare a 212 and a 412. If you're putting the same power into both systems—and you need to be careful, because it's easier to put more power into four 12s—they would sound very similar 40 feet out, but the 412 would sound bigger up close, due to the impedance being lower. It would match the air better, and your ear would hear the power that's in the waveform better. There are other variables, but basically, they'd sound a lot more similar 30 feet away than they would 5 feet away if you're putting the same power into each (and I don't mean same voltage—you've got to put less voltage into the 412 because it's a lower impedance than a 212).

"Interestingly, the speaker area on a 212 is only a little less than a 410. I think it's a really good blend—speaker area for the weight that you're lugging around, the volume of the cabinet—it's actually the best solution for this problem.

"By the way, ports go a long way to changing this whole discussion—and also making it more complicated! What comes out of a port is exactly the kind of wave the ear wants to hear: a low-pressure/high-velocity wave. So if you compare a sealed 112 cabinet with a properly ported 112 cabinet, and get 10 to 15 feet away, you're going to hear the ported cabinet a lot better—the wave will be much better developed. Even up close, you'll hear it a lot better because the energy in that port is the kind of velocity wave that your ear wants to hear.

"The only problem is that oftentimes the ports are down on the floor, and that high-velocity wave just goes right by you and doesn't get a chance to get up to ear level."

Effects

As I mentioned at the outset of this gear discussion, I'm a firm believer that the sound is largely in the hands. One shouldn't expect that the remedy for bad tone is the right foot pedal or high-dollar rack effect unit. It is also less than optimal to be dependent upon such gear when you need a different timbre out of your instruments. I wholeheartedly encourage you to explore and expand your vocabulary of technique so that you can effortlessly transform your sound—from aggressive, driving fingerstyle playing to smooth and clean slapping, or from a muted reggaelike thud to singing, lyrical melodic work—without necessitating a cluster of pedals between your bass and the amp or direct box. A bit of experimentation will quickly reveal that subtle changes in the physical approach to the instrument will yield widely diverse musical statements—for example, which finger or what part of the finger you use to pluck the string, how much pressure you use to pluck, how close or far from the fingerboard you're plucking, how staccato or legato the bass line is being phrased with the fretting hand, if slurring or hammering or vibrato are being employed, and so on.

That said, I love to use effects to supplement the tonal variations afforded by technique. Effects are a fantastic way to enhance a bass line or possibly inspire a player to say something a bit differently, simply due to the sound of the effect. You'd probably alter the way you were phrasing a line if the tone were radically overdriven or distorted, right?

There is a vast spectrum of different types, makes, models, and features of effects available today; a quick perusal through a copy of any of the mail-order music-store catalogs will quickly establish that there's a huge array of options. As has been the case with this entire series, I won't try to discuss every aspect of this topic; rather, I'd like to share with you what I've found most useful—in no particular order.

Chorus/Flanger/Phase Shifters

These three types of effects accomplish their sounds by different means, but the net result is a "swirling" or fluid type of effect. Depending upon the particular unit and how extreme the settings, the effect can range from a subtle singing quality to a very in-your-face, jetlike "swoosh." In terms of worship playing, it is a nice sound with which to experiment when playing long, sustaining notes—particularly higher on the fingerboard—or sometimes when using the slap technique.

Octaver/Pitch Shifters

These effects add a pitch to the note that is being played—most commonly, an octave below. Some units add the note two octaves below or one octave above. Pitch shifters can help you send things to Mars in a hurry, as they readily enable you to add pitches of any interval above or below the played note. It should be noted that this is a fun effect but should be used as a spice only. It can get really old for the listener, and cluttered for the arrangement, if every bass line is a three-octave excursion or involves some sort of clever parallel harmonies. Octavers are great for simulating the sound of synth bass or when playing certain funk lines.

Envelope Filters

Anyone familiar with funk music from the 1970s has heard envelope filters. The "quacking" sound—where each note seems to mutate from one vowel-like tone to another—was made hugely popular by funk pioneers like Bootsy Collins. Perhaps the most popular example of this effect is the Mutron pedal, but there are countless other variations of this unit available today. Most of these effect units are velocity sensitive, which means that the amount of alteration to the sound of the bass is proportional to how hard the note is played. This is another effect that is best used in moderation and with sensitivity to the musical context. As with all effects, the impact of the sound is diminished by overuse.

Overdrive/Distortion

Although a distorted bass tone is undesirable in some musical contexts, there are also occasions when a bit of overdrive is just what the bass needs. In order to achieve this tone while still fulfilling our role of holding down the bottom end, it can be helpful to use a unit designed for bass. This is more critical in the case of distortion, as overdrive effect units designed specifically for bass will feature a crossover, allowing frequencies below a certain point to be unaffected. The fundamental bass tone can then remain intact, while the higher frequencies can be appropriately colored.

Compressors/Limiters

These units control the dynamic range. They can make the loudest notes quieter and the quietest notes louder, or clamp down on the volume such that the loudest notes cannot exceed a certain specified level. The net result is a smoother tone, where the overall volume level can be turned higher because there aren't extreme transients—as is commonly encountered with inexperienced slappers, for instance—to blow up speakers. A certain amount of compression in live and studio settings can fatten up the bass track and help it sit in the mix beautifully.

Anyone familiar with my *Grooving for Heaven* videos will know that I've been fairly outspoken against the use of these units in a bassist's stage setup—the reason being that I hadn't found a pedal unit at that point that didn't thin out the tone. My conclusion was that it was far preferable to leave compression in the hands of the recording or live engineer—who could apply *just* the right amount using *just* the right $4,000 high-end rack unit—and control my dynamic range with my hands.

While I still feel that there's some merit to that, I must also disclose that technology has come a long way and I've since found a pedal compressor unit that does a great job. I tend to use it primarily for fingerstyle rock material, as compression is an integral element of rock bass tone. For other styles of music—particularly funk or fusion, where I will likely employ various percussive techniques—I generally leave compression to the engineer and control dynamic range with technique. It's really not all that hard to do, and it gives me the freedom to lay into that one phrase that really needs to jump out without being slammed down by the compression "Threshold of Doom"!

Equalizers

When looking over the huge variety of equalizers on the market, I consider the primary variable to be whether the unit is *graphic* or *parametric*. Graphic equalizers are similar to your home stereo, where there are faders assigned to individual frequencies, and they can each be boosted or cut as needed. These tend to be the most intuitive for the average player. Parametric equalizers allow much more precise tone shaping; the frequency or frequencies can be selected, and the width of the adjacent frequencies to be altered can be set—this is typically referred to as the Q—and subsequently boosted or cut. Parametric EQ can be good in the right hands or problematic in the wrong.

The above is an extreme simplification; volumes have been written on this topic by many great engineers, and I urge you to research further if interested. My perspectives have evolved through many years of playing in both live and session environments. In general, I recommend limiting the amount of equalization to the absolute minimum necessary to achieve your desired tone—particularly when boosting high frequencies, as much additional noise or hiss can be introduced into the signal path by improper use of equalizers. Additionally, drastic EQ settings might sound good where you're standing but often don't correspond to what is needed in the overall mix. Also, my earlier remarks regarding technique are perhaps most applicable to equalization: a bassist can achieve big variations simply by altering the manner in which the note is being played.

Have fun exploring the world of effects, and always remember to use them as an *enhancement* to an already solid tone!

Espresso Time...
with Dominique Di Piazza

Fans of jazz fusion will recognize Dominique as the bassist on the phenomenal John McLaughlin album *Que Alegria*. His amazing command and innovative approach to the bass—as demonstrated by blazing unison runs with John, sublime chordal work, and ridiculously swinging walking lines—sent many a bassist running to the proverbial woodshed.

Dominique has been a friend of mine since approximately 2001. The following are excerpts from a conversation we had around that time. I was blown away by the humility and graciousness that flows from this absolute monster of a musician—who became a Christian shortly after his stint with McLaughlin.

Born in Lyon, France, Di Piazza currently divides his time between Paris and the South of France. Due to space constraints, only highlights from the interview have been compiled here. For a full transcript of the conversation covering Dominique's truly inspiring life and testimony, visit www.normstockton.com.

THE EARLY YEARS

My father, a Sicilian—my mother is French—left when I was young, and my mother remarried a man who was a Gypsy. My earliest musical exposure was to his Gypsy music. I also was exposed to a lot of other ethnic styles, such as African, flamenco, Indian, Eastern European music from Romania and Russia, as well as some from the Orient. I began to play the guitar when I was about 15. Around the age of 18, I started listening to a lot of bebop and other jazz. When I first heard Weather Report's *Heavy Weather*—with Jaco—I decided to focus on being a bass player. It really reminded me of the upbeat African music that I used to listen to.

ON CONNECTING WITH JOHN MCLAUGHLIN

I was playing in a famous jazz club in Paris. I knew a magazine columnist who liked my playing. He came up one evening and said that he was going to be interviewing John McLaughlin the following week and asked if I had a recording of one of my solos that he could pass on to John. All I had was a little cassette tape recorded live on a Walkman, but I gave it to him and more or less forgot about it. Well, my columnist friend ended up giving the tape to John and said, "You must listen to this guy." John receives tapes like this almost every day from people who want to play with him. He put my cassette in a box with a bunch of other tapes for the tour-bus driver. Well, his driver—who was more into rock music—eventually got around to my tape and put it in the tape player with the volume set very high. [*Laughs.*] The bus driver was trying to turn it off because it wasn't rock! But John told him to wait and listened to the recording. When it was done, John pulled it out of the tape player and called my phone number—which my columnist friend had written on the cassette case. So I received a phone call, and the voice on the other line had an English accent—which I thought was a friend of mine trying to be funny! Well, this was a time in my life when I was chasing gigs and had no money—very hard time. So anyway, the man said, "I am John McLaughlin, and I listened to your cassette." I replied, "Okay, I know it's you, Stefan (a drummer friend), and do you know that Miles Davis just called you up yesterday and he wants to hire you!" [*Laughs.*] But the guy on the other line kept insisting, saying, "I've listened to your cassette and I'm interested in meeting you—I thought it was very good." Finally, the man quoted the name of the journalist who had given him the tape! "Oooohhhh!" I said, "Okay, uh, John. I thought you were . . ."

TORTURE THROUGH AUDITION

I knew that he played tunes like "Giant Steps," and at that time I was very proud of what I could do—so I was very at ease as we played through that tune and a number of other Coltrane songs. When we were done, he said, "Okay, now we're going to try something in 5/8." 5/8? [*Laughs.*] I didn't even know how to count it! After we played through that piece, he proceeded to call out a tune in 9/8! As we played through, I was watching his foot tapping and was completely lost! After that, I was telling myself, "Okay, he doesn't need to speak a word. I know that this is not going to happen." But he told me that he'd give me the record and we'd meet in about six months to play through the songs again, perhaps with Trilok Gurtu—the legendary percussionist. For the following six months, I revived my past way of practicing—12 to 15 hours per day—but this time it was useful! But I'm not a good reader—although I know harmony and chords very well, I can't properly read music—so I couldn't read the music I was practicing. I was trying so hard to understand what Trilok was doing. [*Hums a scarily syncopated and rhythmically nebulous groove.*] I was just sitting there, thinking, "What?!" [Laughs.]

Anyway, six months later, I went to do the audition and I was green—my actual skin color was green! I was washing my hands every five minutes from the sweat. But it all worked out.

UNORTHODOX TECHNIQUE

When I first started playing bass, I didn't know proper bass technique, so my technique was a combination of pick playing—from my guitar background—and fingerstyle. It used to be very difficult for me because people couldn't accept my approach to the instrument. At that time, John Patitucci was not known in France, and the only other similar player known in that country was perhaps Jeff Berlin. My right-hand technique is mainly picking with two fingers: my thumb and middle finger. I sometimes add my index finger so I can play triplet figures. This developed because I already had a lot of bebop music in my head before I started playing bass—you know, all of those arpeggios; I really like arpeggios—and I found that the easiest way to play them was with this technique. I also use a lot of left-hand hammer-ons, pull-offs, and slides in conjunction with my picking technique. But for the fast, staccato playing, it is mainly two fingers.

FRONT PAGE

Front Page is the name of both the new [c. 2001] CD and the trio that features Bireli Lagrene (guitar), Dennis Chambers (drums), and me. John McLaughlin is also featured on one track. It should be available in US record stores before the end of the year. There's an interesting story surrounding this album. Bireli wrote about half of the tunes for this project, and I wrote the others. Many of my songs had titles that referred to the Lord. Particularly, I felt led to name this one song "The Eyes of Jesus Christ." Well, when we were in the studio recording the project, the manager was really giving me a hard time about the title. It got so heated that I left the studio to take a walk. I really wanted to not react in the flesh and get angry. To make a long story short, the head of the record company was also pressuring me to change that title, saying, "We can live with the other titles, but we really want you to change this one song name." I just felt that I wasn't supposed to give in, so I didn't. I didn't know until the CD was actually manufactured that they ended up keeping my titles! The project ended up doing quite well in France—receiving a nomination for France's equivalent to a Grammy award. We were up against a very popular artist who had sold very, very well in France, and we were being told that we didn't have a chance. But we had a prayer meeting, and people at my church ended up renting me a suit, loaning me a car, and giving me a bit of money to get to Paris to attend the awards show. When I arrived, people were asking me why I was there, since it was already pretty much decided that the other artist was going to win. But when they announced the winner, it was our group!

GEAR OF DOMINIQUE

When I was playing with John, I had a Warwick Streamer five-string and a Kubicki Factor four-string. I am presently using Noguera basses made by a French luthier. I have two—both five-strings, tuned EADGC. One is fretted, and the other is fitted with a special bridge system I made myself that gives it a fretless sound—sort of halfway between a sitar and a fretless bass [*Dominique has since become an endorser for Mike Sabre basses*]. It can be heard on the new Front Page album coming out in the States, on the tune "The Eyes of Jesus Christ." I also endorse Warwick's Pro Tube 9 amp, Line 6's Bass Pod, and Lakewood Guitars—since I'm starting to play guitar again.

THE PRODIGAL RETURNS

I came from a divorced family, so I was hurting as a child. When I was 11 years old, I was at a camp in Switzerland where they explained to me the plan of salvation for the first time. I realized that I was a sinner. I was a bad boy, in a way, because I was hurting so badly ever since my father left—but I discovered that God loves me, that He died for me. So this was in my heart, but I fell away after that.

Well, at that time, I was on tour all the time. For me, music was everything. I thought that I would be satisfied when I played with big musicians and became a big musician myself—with money and fame. But something was missing. So I got married, and that was very good. But after a while, between the responsibility and the routine of daily life, it didn't seem as good as it was at first. After two years, I had toured around the world. I had money. I was playing with John McLaughlin. I knew Chick Corea and many other guys like that. And I wasn't satisfied. It was around that time that I began to realize that there was darkness inside of me, and I wondered what I could do.

In 1992, a drummer friend came to dinner at my house. My wife and I had been married for about one year. He shared his faith, and it reminded me of what I'd heard when I was a kid—and my wife got saved! [*Laughs.*] Praise the Lord. She was born again before my eyes. After that, she spoke of Jesus Christ and the Bible all the time.

One day, I went to find a quiet place and I went into a small church in Paris. I began to think about my past and realized that I was heavily burdened. I started reflecting on the words of the Lord from that Take 6 song: "Come unto Me, and I will give you rest." So in a way, God spoke to me in English! As I looked at the Cross, I realized that God hadn't changed, but that I had. I asked God why my father had left home. It was the hurt of my life. But I could hear Him answering me as He drew my eyes to the Cross: "And why did My Son have to die?" I could feel a struggle going on inside me. Finally, I wept, and I told Him, "God, I want to know You more. I want to follow You. I want to receive like my wife. Do something if You're really there." And you know, I immediately started to feel peace, and hope, and when I walked in the door, my wife looked in my eyes and knew I was changed. I was not the same anymore. I was not the same anymore!

ON BEING A CHRISTIAN AND A MUSICIAN

On one level, I've come to find that there can be an anointing on even instrumental music. God can bless music and touch people through it. I also believe that music can really be evangelistic. I've also found that you can be both a Christian and a good musician. In France, there's a mentality that if you're a Christian, then you can't be a good player. They picture a Salvation Army street band—that sort of thing. I understand now as a Christian that music comes from God and He is the Giver of gifts—so it is an expression of praise now when I play music. I've been freed to really enjoy myself now as a musician, much more than before. As I mentioned earlier, I used to have a really bad self-image as a musician because of the resistance I faced playing bass the way I do. But now I feel the liberty to be the musician God created me to be: who is to say that the bass has to be played like this, or that it has to sound like that? I now can say that I am this way by the grace of God, and although I know I can't play everything that others do, what I play—my own little thing—it's me. Even when I first started playing music as a Christian, I only wanted to play really soft, you know. [*Hums long drones with lots of vibrato.*] And it was like I could hear the Lord quietly asking, "*What* are you doing?!" [*Laughs.*] But I'd also say that being a musician is not my identity. I know that my identity is in Christ; I first became a disciple before I began playing music again. So my real identity, or self-image, is in Christ. I think that's really important.

FINAL ENCOURAGEMENT

Pursue excellence in the way that God deserves. Why do we let the world do the best work or the most serious work, you know? It's sad to say, but many players in the church today, if they were playing out in the world, would be fired. That's sometimes a reason why people in the world mock or laugh. I'm not saying that everyone has to be a virtuoso, but what they do has to be...with a servant's heart, the best it can be and really serving the tune. We should be really diligent, attentive to others, and really try to develop and improve.

Visit Dominique at www.dominiquedipiazza.com

A SELECTED DISCOGRAPHY

- John McLaughlin: *Que Alegria*
- Michael Blass: *Wait and See*
- Louis Vinsberg Trio: *Camino*
- Gil Evans: *Lumiere*
- Dominique Di Piazza: *Spiritual Hymns*

5

Tips for the Woodshed

Most of you are probably already aware that "spending time in the woodshed"—or woodshedding, for short—is musician-speak for practicing. The following tips and suggestions relative to your practice time are nuggets that I've found highly beneficial in my own musical development, as well as that of private students and clinic attendees—but it is definitely not a comprehensive list of all pertinent considerations for practicing. If there are areas of your musicianship that you feel are underdeveloped and not included in this chapter, I encourage you to spend time focusing on those specific areas regardless.

It should be noted that many of the ideas aren't unique to me, and I'll make every effort to appropriately credit—as my overextended memory allows!

Warm-Ups

Having dealt with tendinitis over the years, I'm acutely aware of the need for a proper warm-up routine prior to playing. Countless well-intentioned players have incurred catastrophic—that is to say, career- and/or worship ministry–ending—damage to arms and hands by neglecting to get a little blood flowing prior to commencing upon a bombastic musical excursion. I was perilously close to being one of them, and it is my profound desire that you might learn from my mistakes!

Two of the most effective and easy warm-ups are:

1.   With palms facing up, bend each consecutive finger—one at a time—up
      and touch the fingertip to your palm. It looks a bit like Spider-Man's hand
      position when shooting a web for those who need a visual. The movement
      should be primarily limited to the joint where the fingers attach to the
      hand, with the fingers being kept relatively straight for most of the motion.

2.   Again with palms facing up, bring your fingers up in pairs—first the
      first and third fingers, then the second and fourth, alternating back and
      forth—and use your thumbs to briefly hold them to their respective palms
      (random bonus content: there's a great indie band name—the Respective
      Palms!) With each pair of fingers, stretch the two extended fingers—the
      ones not being held down by the thumb—away from your palms for a
      moment. Then switch to the other pair and repeat. I first heard of this
      stretch through bass icon Stu Hamm and I believe he got it from studio
      bass pioneer Carol Kaye. It works fantastically.

Both of these stretching exercises can be done during the commute to your gig—one
hand at a time while driving, of course!—so you'll be warmed up and ready to shake the
rafters immediately upon plugging into your amp at the venue.

Practicing Time

Developing a consistent and accurate internal sense of time is one of the key objectives
for any bassist. The good news is that one doesn't have to emerge from the womb with
good time; it's something that can be developed with practice. How does one develop this
"internal clock"? By spending time on a regular basis working in a focused manner with a
real clock—a metronome, that is.

This is another of the crucial "eating-your-veggies" aspects of musicianship: it's neither
flashy nor particularly fun—at least initially—but there is arguably no more effective means
for taking your bass playing up to the next level. Consistent work with a metronome will
reap huge dividends as it gradually calibrates your internal sense of time.

The note pitches aren't important for these exercises; as a matter of fact, muting the strings with your fretting hand, so that the notes sound like thuds, will better enable you to focus on rhythmic accuracy. It is, however, really helpful to practice playing those thuds on alternating strings. I encourage you to mix it up and be creative—and yes, if you're *dying* to hear something harmonic, put your fretting hand to work and incorporate scales, modes, arpeggios, and so on. Just ensure that it doesn't distract from the primary focus on rhythm.

These are some of my favorites:

1. This one's from David Hungate, the legendary original bassist with Toto and first-call Nashville session player: set your metronome to 40 bpm, which will probably be the slowest setting on most electronic metronomes. Try to play staccato quarter notes between each click, with the click sounding on beat 1 of each measure. Listen for any *flams*, or instances when the click and your bass aren't precisely together (they will sound like "bloom" versus "boom") and try to adjust your playing accordingly. This exercise is surprisingly tough yet amazingly helpful—primarily because the metronome isn't providing any subdivision, so you are reliant upon your own internal clock to keep time between each click. With practice, you'll gradually be able to lock—or play in sync—with the click sooner and sooner.

2. Set the metronome click at 90 bpm—these will be quarter notes sounding on each downbeat. Get used to tapping your foot on each click—count "one, two, three, four" to help internalize the quarter-note pulse—and practice playing measures of:

   - whole notes
   - half notes
   - quarter notes
   - eighth notes
   - sixteenth notes
   - quarter-note triplets (6 notes per measure)
   - eighth-note triplets (12 notes per measure)
   - sixteenth-note triplets (24 notes per measure—if your fingers can accommodate the request!)

Once you're comfortable with each subdivision, practice mixing them up and alternating between them. As you do this, pay close attention to ensure that you're not rushing or dragging the tempo—particularly during the first few beats of each new rhythmic pattern.

3. Play with the metronome clicks on only beats 1 and 3 at a variety of tempos (hint: reduce the metronome's bpm setting to half of the intended tempo). Then, leaving the same metronome setting, hear the clicks as beats 2 and 4, and practice grooving with those clicks serving as the backbeat.

4. Play that first exercise (the one from David Hungate) with the metronome click on beat 2 only. Then go back and play with it on beat 3. Then beat 4. Isn't it interesting how our perception of the feel is radically altered depending upon where we are hearing the click? This is *great stuff*.

5. Set the metronome to 90 bpm again—have you discerned yet that it's my favorite tempo?—and practice alternating back and forth between a measure of straight sixteenth notes and a measure of shuffled (per Figure 6-8 in the "Musical Styles" chapter) sixteenth notes. Listen for flams or other rhythmic inconsistencies!

Have fun and groove hard!

Ear Training

It's been said that the distinction between a great musician and a lesser player lies not in how fast one can play but rather in how fast one can *listen*. So true! Developing our ears to the extent that we can quickly and accurately discern, identify, and respond to elements of the music—harmonic, melodic, rhythmic, and so on—is one of the most important musical areas in which we can invest our time and energy.

I'd like to focus on the following specific areas of ear training.

Intervals

In the "Fingerboard Familiarity" chapter, I briefly discussed intervals. You'll recall that the interval system is a numbering system based upon the notes of the major scale. Harmonically, the C major scale is defined by the notes C, D, E, F, G, A, B, C. But intervallically, it is defined as 1, 2, 3, 4, 5, 6, 7, 8 (octave). Any deviations from the relationship of a certain interval to the root (the "1") would be addressed as a sharp or flat—for example, if the seventh were played a half step lower than its normal placement found in the major scale, it would be identified as a flatted-seventh, or flat-seventh, or ♭7.

It is extremely valuable for any musician, especially a bassist, to have the ability to hear and identify these intervals in the octaves both above and below a particular note. This will be a huge help in allowing a player to musically dialogue with other players in the ensemble spontaneously.

A really great exercise to further develop and assimilate this involves playing a random note on the bass, then singing the desired interval relative to that note—say, the fifth above. Great vocal chops aren't required here, by the way—just the ability to *hear* the note clearly in your head. Then, play the fifth above on the bass and verify if it was the note you were singing. Repeat for all of the intervals in both the octave above and octave below, and practice them in random order.

Beat Placement

The better we are at hearing and identifying rhythmic ideas in a drum groove, the better equipped we will be to function effectively in a rhythm section. Spend time listening to drum loops or sequenced drum parts and identify the beat placement of each instrument—closed versus open hi-hat, kick, snare, toms, ride, crashes, and so on. Learn what various rhythmic ideas sound like. Learn to identify common rhythmic concepts or patterns, and be able to sing them over the top of drum grooves that might not be implying them—for example, sing a shuffled rhythm over a straight drum groove, or sing eighth- or sixteenth-note anticipations over loops that don't have those pushes, and so on.

Learning Tunes by Ear

Educational purists sometimes seem to look down upon this method of learning music, but I am convinced that it is one of the most effective ways to develop those listening skills we seek. I wholeheartedly encourage you to regularly invest time in learning tunes—or portions of tunes, solos, and so on—by ear. Listen to a short segment, pause the CD or MP3 player, sing that musical phrase, and find it on your bass.

You'll quickly discover that it's a real-life application involving both of the elements of ear training I just covered!

Chart Reading

Although I'll be addressing this topic in detail in the "Chart Fundamentals" chapter, I would be remiss if I didn't include a mention in this woodshed section. Suffice it to say that learning to read music is *invaluable*. It opens up a whole world of instructional resources to you. Additionally, if music is your current or potential vocation, you're radically limiting your employment opportunities by not reading.

The good news is that it really isn't that hard. Sure it takes time and requires consistent practice in order to be functional, but getting to the point where you can navigate your way through a normal rhythm chart isn't beyond any player's abilities. Learn what some common rhythms look like when written out. Learn basic roadmap signs—repeats, DCs, DSs, codas—as well as dynamic and phrasing marks. Most of all, read often; consistency is the key.

Assimilating Techniques

There are numerous techniques utilized in contemporary bass playing, including slapping, tapping, and so on. Many of these techniques are quite amazing to witness in the hands of a tasteful player. However, it should be mentioned that using these techniques as the basis and foundation for your musicianship ultimately limits the depth and substance of your artistry. I'm discussing these advanced techniques in the context of the player who already possesses a solid understanding of the role of the bassist in the ensemble. Learning to tap or slap should be down on the priority list from learning to groove, learning basic harmony, expanding your vocabulary of styles, and so on.

That stated, once a foundation of musicianship is established, I wholeheartedly encourage you to explore the range of available techniques and even innovate upon them. As far as getting them under your fingers, I have found it very helpful to first learn the basic technique out of time—without worrying about metronomic accuracy. For example, when I've worked on expanding my vocabulary of slap techniques, some of the right-hand motions were so unfamiliar, particularly with some of the double-thumbing, that it took me a while to get to the point where my fingers could even successfully execute the motion. Once it was fairly comfortable and I could employ the technique consistently, then it was time to put in the hours with a metronome and drum machine to refine it.

Please ensure that you always warm up prior to working on this sort of technique and avoid spending too much time working on one repetitive motion before taking a break or working on something that involves a different motion. Tendinitis and other playing-related injuries thrive on the "no pain no gain" mentality that many well-intentioned musicians bring to the woodshed.

Developing Your Vocabulary

One of the best things musicians can do is develop and expand their musical vocabularies. It seems that the most effective and capable players have a seemingly bottomless bag from which they draw their musical ideas. Whether the tune calls for funk, driving rock, a delicate ballad treatment, straight-ahead jazz, Latin, or any of the countless other musical genres or variants, they seem to always have just the right musical statements to contribute.

How did they develop that ability? While I definitely believe that great musicians are born with God-given talents for their artistic expression and ability, I also believe that those who reach a high level of excellence are the ones who have put in the effort and time to faithfully invest in those talents—in other words, tons of time in the woodshed. That principal absolutely applies to this matter of developing a musical vocabulary.

I encourage you to make time in your schedule for active analytical listening to lots of different music from diverse genres. Listen, and try to determine what characteristics—rhythmic, harmonic, melodic, and sonic—really define that style, particularly with regard to the bass line. Once you've identified those idioms of a certain musical style, work to assimilate them into your own vocabulary.

Are there certain licks that truly typify that genre? Make them your own by tweaking them in some way to personalize them. Once you feel that you've achieved a general understanding of a particular genre, move on to another! This method has been used by countless great players to stunning effect.

Much more on this topic in the upcoming "Crash Course: Musical Styles" chapter.

Taking It to the Next Level

To assimilate these styles to the extent that you can spontaneously draw from them on the gig, I recommend practicing by playing through familiar tunes using *unfamiliar* styles and grooves. A drum machine or sequencer with lots of preset grooves in a variety of styles—or many software solutions, such as Apple's GarageBand—will help facilitate this.

For example, if there's a song you've played through a million times as a slow pop ballad (you know the one I'm talking about!), program your drum machine or sequencer to play a reggae groove and try to negotiate the tune in that style. By the way, please take note that I'm talking about an exercise for your woodshed time: I'm not necessarily advocating turning a worship ballad into a thrash-funkfest this coming Sunday morning—unless that will help the tune communicate the lyric more effectively. Perhaps your worship leader or musical director will be a good resource to speak to this! But for your personal practice time, the aforementioned ballad funkification is a fabulous idea.

Other suggestions for this exercise include playing tunes that are normally played straight as shuffles (or vice versa), or songs normally in 3/4 as 4/4 (or vice versa), and so on. Anything that focuses on application of your expanding groove vocabulary—especially in ways that aren't necessarily comfortable or second-nature to you yet—is incredibly helpful for developing the ability to apply your knowledge freely and confidently in an actual playing environment.

Playing What You Mean

I frequently make reference to the "FedEx approach" to bass playing (absolutely no offense to Federal Express—I use them all the time—but I think you'll see the point): it involves the bassist delivering an unimpassioned bass line with sort of a "you ordered sixteen measures of eighth notes in E minor can you sign right here please" mentality. The bass line is executed, but is devoid of any emotional impact or artistic communication whatsoever.

I've obviously already covered this topic in some detail (see "The Spice" chapter), but I would like to challenge those of you who might be identifying with this to continue working toward truly communicating on your bass. After all, our role as instrumentalists is to communicate with the listener. And as I mentioned, for those of us who are worship musicians, it goes even deeper—to the point that the instrumentalists seek to help the song convey what is happening lyrically and spiritually at any given moment.

From a technical standpoint, remember that this involves more than just feeling strongly about your bass line. In addition to the actual notes and rhythms being played, it really boils down to all of those phrasing variables: note duration, dynamics, slurs/hammers, vibrato, register, and so on. You'll recall that variations in those elements, whether applied to spoken words or music, can make the same statement convey entirely different sentiments.

One final exercise I'd like to share to help get you thinking more along the lines of singing and emoting your bass parts involves turning down the volume on your television and musically responding to the various stimuli. Or providing a musical soundtrack to what you're watching. Is it a sappy made-for-TV movie? Provide appropriately sappy accompaniment. Is it a fuel-storage facility being blown to smithereens as the hero or heroine leaps to safety at the last possible instant? Play something heroic. None of the musical statements have to be long: sometimes one or two notes with just the right amount of angst, tenderness, or queasiness will say everything that needs to be said. Have fun!

Woodshed Schedule

Having a good local teacher—who teaches *music*, as opposed to "Okay, now play *this* lick…."— is optimal. That person can assess your specific strengths and *areas of potential growth*, and prescribe exercises targeting those areas. If you don't have a good teacher in your area, or you'd otherwise prefer to study with me, you're also invited to join me at my online lesson site: www.ArtOfGroove.com.

As far as a practice schedule goes, it's obviously difficult for me to fully assess the optimal balance of time for your specific needs, but here's a general recommendation for time allotment:

- **Warm Up:** At least three minutes.
- **Reading and Theory:** 30 percent.
- **Technique:** 30 percent.
- **Working on Time/Groove/Feel:** 30 percent.
- **End with Something Fun:** 10 percent.

By the way, you'll notice that much of the material I've thrown your way in this chapter can easily fall under multiple categories in this breakdown; that's actually great! For instance, if you can work on reading, technique, and theory at the same time, more power to you.

The proportions are basic guidelines that can be adapted for the amount of time your schedule will allow. Additionally, there will sometimes be more of one thing and less of another. The key is to practice every day; four hours every other Saturday won't result in consistent progress.

Lastly, try to focus no less than half of your time on areas that are difficult for you. Woodshedding things that you already do well isn't nearly as productive as consistent repetition on musical areas that kick your tail. It's not quite as much fun, but your musical development will definitely reflect your hard work!

Let's Grab Coffee: Play a Part

Although my initial desire to be a bassist was sparked by Paul McCartney's playing on the Beatles' classics, I essentially learned to play by emulating the playing of a certain progressive rock bassist who is famous for a riff-oriented, generally busy style of playing. Consequently, my playing for years was a series of guitarlike, unrelated, and random—albeit harmonically and technically correct—snippets. Although certain genres and musical contexts may lend themselves to constant variation in the bass line—avant-garde improvisational music comes to mind—the overwhelming majority of the music most of us find ourselves playing calls for a different musical approach.

My older brother, Ray—a musical mentor in the early years—used to talk to me about establishing a motif, or "repetition with variation," also sometimes referred to as *theme and variation*. It took me many years before I truly appreciated the importance of his point. It boils down to how people hear music.

Let me illustrate with an example I use in my clinics. I play several times through a chord progression comprising two bars of A minor and two bars of G major. In version 1, I randomly noodle a variety of licks within that chord structure. In version 2, I play the bass line from the intro of the Police's "Walking on the Moon." I then challenge anyone to try to sing back to me, by memory, any portion of the bass line from version 1.

Invariably, and quite understandably, no one can remember the slightest thing about such a collection of random statements as the first version. It lacked any apparent intent or direction; there was simply nothing to sink your teeth into. Version 2, on the other hand, is an easily assimilated phrase, instantly recognizable when the song returns to that bass figure after the B-section.

Ray's point was that most effective bass lines—and most effective music in general—involve a specific figure or motif that is somewhat repetitive. This repetition serves to establish a foundation for the tune, giving the listener something to grasp, and then progressively incorporates variations as the tune develops.

I encourage you to go back and analytically listen to some of your favorite music and see if you hear this concept employed, not only by the bass but by the other instruments as well. I believe you'll find countless examples.

Try to come up with a one- or two-bar part for each section of the tunes you play. Your drummer will be elated to have a consistent rhythmic figure with which to play, and you'll find the overall arrangement of the tunes enhanced.

I feel that applying this approach to my bass playing was one of the most important factors in my own musical development—*thanks, Ray!* I'm confident you'll find the same to be true for you.

6

Crash Course: Musical Styles

Familiarity with a broad range of musical styles is invaluable for any bassist. One of the most effective ways we can bring freshness to our playing is through various stylistic influences. Even if our usual musical outlets might not be particularly receptive to excursions into reggae, blues, or thrash-funk, having a basic understanding of those and other styles can liberate and equip us when it's time to be creative.

While I'm on the topic, though, I know many of you have experienced varying degrees of frustration with the narrowing range of musical styles encountered in much of worship music today.

I get it. I honestly do. Please let me offer the following perspectives for your consideration:

- Musical trends are cyclical. It's just a matter of time before other genres and musical approaches make their way to Sunday morning.
- It's my role to do everything I can to serve and help the song say what the song needs to say. If a tune calls for whole notes from the bass, I want to provide them with the best possible feel and emotion that I'm capable of conveying. The last thing I want to do is impose my own personal musical preferences (West African grooves? Jazz licks? Funk embellishments?) upon a song that's written and arranged otherwise, relegating my part to be a "check me out" statement, at best, and likely a distraction to band and congregation.

- I urge you to not let the worship service be your only outlet for musical expression. Whether it's playing with other bands or just recording little jams at home on your iPhone, exploring the vast diversity of music is a fantastic idea and invaluable for your growth and creative fulfillment as a musician. But the worship time is about serving.

- Every musical genre requires skill and familiarity with its idioms to play well. Players who experience boredom playing rock eighth notes, for instance, usually aren't digging into the subtleties enough to play them with the correct feel and phrasing. To enjoy any musical style that might not initially interest you, I encourage you to take the time to explore these subtleties and strive to really convey that style with musical and emotional authenticity. You'll have more fun and will undoubtedly discover there's more to it than what was immediately apparent.

Cool? Anyway, let's dive back in!

Something I frequently mention in clinics bears repeating here: a Latin bass line is not simply a country bass line played while wearing a sombrero. There are specific musical elements that are idiomatic of a genre. In order to really have a particular style in our bass vocabularies, it's important to have a fundamental knowledge of some of those idioms. In other words, it's essential that we assimilate what technical things make a style of music sound that way; I refer to it as "What makes the funk *funky?*" Those idioms may be rhythmic, harmonic, melodic, or even sonic—tone, instrumental choices, and so on.

Let's briefly evaluate a handful of different styles of music and identify some of those idioms from the bassist's perspective. I'd like to encourage you to use these genre studies as a springboard for your own personal analysis of other styles of music—perhaps your favorites as well as some new discoveries. Try to identify some of the idioms of those other musical styles, then work to assimilate them. They can then be part of your musical palette.

I'll keep the chord progression fairly generic, simple, and consistent for all of these examples so that you can really focus in on the idioms themselves:

- 2 bars of G
- 2 bars of C
- 1 bar each of Am (A-) and D
- back to G

The last bar of the progression will usually go back to the V chord, D (or D7, Dsus, Dadd4, and so on), before repeating in bars 9 to 16.

As a final preface, I do want to say that I was reluctant to include tablature in the written examples because I strongly feel that developing reading skills using standard notation is infinitely preferable; you won't walk into too many playing situations where tunes are charted using tablature. However, I recognized that excluding it would have left many of you unable to participate. So if necessary, please use the tab to assist you in negotiating the written line above it, and then work to wean yourself!

Okay! Let's take a look at the first genre.

Country

Figure 6-1. Country.

You're probably already aware that the country feel generally calls for a simple, straightforward type of bass line that is really solid and foundational. Rhythmically, it usually sticks closely with the kick-drum pattern. In this example, the drum groove would generally have a simple eighth-note feel or subdivision with light kick drum on beats 1, 3, and the *and* of beat 2. You can see that the bass part definitely lines up with that kick pattern.

I threw in a couple of things that are signature country bass licks; you'll probably recognize some of them right away. There's the traditional country bass walk-up, going from the I chord to the IV chord in bar 2, or from the V chord back to the I chord in bar 6 (you'll notice that I also habitually throw in the fifth on the last eighth note—completely optional!) That line can also be frequently found in country tunes as a pick-up at the beginning of the song, where it can imply the V chord leading to the I chord.

Otherwise, country bass lines are generally not characterized by a lot of tense passing tones. Usually, they're fairly inside, harmonically, using scale tones—lots of roots and fifths. Save those tension notes for your jazz gig!

Tonally, you won't usually hear a lot of treble "clack" in the bass tone. A warm, round tone with solid bottom and low-mids is normally the best choice.

I encourage you to experiment with this style. It's actually somewhat deceptive—some of you may read or hear a bass line like this and think to yourself, "What a *breeze*!!"—but to play it with impeccable feel, good phrasing, and unwavering time takes a high level of musicianship.

Jazz

Figure 6-2. Jazz.

Here's a bit of a jazzier take on that chord progression (Figure 6-2). You'll notice that I opted to go for more of a loose, jazz-ballad type of feel versus a traditional walking quarter-note approach. Aside from the fact that there are innumerable fantastic volumes already out there for learning the art of jazz walking, I've also found that a jazz-ballad treatment (particularly if done subtly) can sometimes more easily be incorporated into a worship setting (code for "under the radar"!) Walking lines can tend to give it that "Charlie Parker Does Worship" kind of vibe—which can be great, too, if you've got a ministry situation where that would be appropriate. If you want to split the difference, though, perhaps experiment with the type of approach I've taken here.

Figure 6-3. Swing eighth notes.

Please note that the eighth notes are swung (Figure 6-3) and should be phrased accordingly.

As far as the idioms that make it a jazz bass line: the chromatic approach tones are very typical jazz bass signatures; note the use of chromaticism in bars 2, 4, 5, 6, and so on. It is common to approach the next chord by either walking up or down from a half step or whole step above or below the target root note.

Additionally, incorporating a II–V cadence (instead of just the V chord) as a turnaround is a very typical convention of the genre, so I've included that in bar 8. If the other instrumentalists are agreeable, an extended turnaround over the last two bars of the progression (bars 7–8 or 15–16) would also be a common jazz signature. It sometimes doesn't work as well if the other harmonic instruments aren't also implying that chord motion. There are countless variations of the turnaround:

- IIIm7–VI7–IIm7–V7
- IM7–♭III7–II7–♭II7
- IM7–♭IIIM7–♭VIM7–♭IIM7

Rhythmically, the overall vibe is very much to phrase things on the back of the beat; it tends to give it the requisite feel. If this passage were played with everything really on top—pushing, or slightly ahead—of the beat, it would introduce a sense of urgency contradictory to what we're really trying to achieve by this stylistic approach.

In terms of the sound, this sort of jazz ballad generally calls for a very warm tone emulating an upright bass. You'll probably want to roll off the treble knob somewhat and play in a manner where you're not getting a lot of fret noise—or better yet, break out your fretless bass.

If you'd like to explore this genre, I'd highly encourage you to listen to some of the masters of jazz bass: Ron Carter, Ray Brown, Paul Chambers, and many others. You can learn volumes about the style by analyzing and emulating their playing on any of the jazz classics.

Funk

Now try applying a bit of a fingerstyle funk approach to the chord progression. Here's one possible version (Figure 6-4):

Figure 6-4. Funk.

And here's a different example that's more of a single-chord vamp (Figure 6-5):

Figure 6-5. Funk vamp.

You might notice the use of a thematic approach: repetition is employed to establish the motif or part in both versions. In Figure 6-4, the bass line in bar 3 and 4 is just a transposed version of the bass line in bar 1 and 2, while bars 1 and 3 in Figure 6-5 are identical. Variations are then introduced as the tune progresses.

In terms of funk idioms that are employed, this thematic approach is actually very common for this sort of funk groove: a syncopated, staccato repetitive bass line with occasional variations characterizes many classic fingerstyle funk lines.

Rhythmically, the sixteenth-note pulse that's created using a combination of ghost notes and voiced notes is definitely an idiom of the style as well. Bassists will typically spontaneously pick and choose where they're going to play actual pitched notes, while much of the rest of the line is filled with ghosted eighth and sixteenth notes.

Harmonically, funk grooves will often use certain passing or chromatic approach tones and target notes. In the groove examples, they're generally incorporated into the bass lines using slurs or hammers.

Common examples in funk include:

- 6 to ♭7
- ♭3 to major 3
- ♯5 to 6
- ♯4 to 5
- ♭5 to 4

A number of different musical styles—funk, jazz, and blues come to mind—also employ chromatic approach in similar ways. It introduces the characteristic tension and resolution that is such an essential part of those genres.

By the way, as I mentioned at the beginning of this chapter: in the interest of minimizing variables and distinguishing between genre idioms versus the arrangement, the chord progression in Figure 6.4 is consistent with the individual style studies in this series. In real-world application, many of the chord qualities there would have been tweaked to include more dominant chords and color tones—which in turn would have facilitated more of the aforementioned passing tones.

Tonally, it's truly a matter of preference; some bassists might elect to go for an upper midrange-heavy Jazz-bass tone, while others might gravitate toward a warmer P-bass thud. My personal taste tends more toward the latter; it settles easily into a mix, propels the band well, and has solid bottom end that stays nicely below the range of the other instruments. This can be helpful for avoiding an excessively cluttered arrangement.

The term *funk* (like *rock*) describes a really broad range of music. These examples cover one of countless possible funk approaches. That said, if one were to make a general statement about the essence of the style, it would be safe to say that it's music with "attitude." If a bass groove sounds corny, it's most likely not very authentic in the funk sense!

As always, listen to the masters of the style—Francis Rocco Prestia, Marcus Miller, Bootsy Collins, and many others—and use this study as a starting point for your own funk exploration!

Latin

The term *Latin music*—perhaps to an even greater extent than *rock* or *funk*—describes an enormously diverse range of music, particularly with respect to bass grooves.

Here is an example using a very common Latin bass figure called the *tumbao* (Figure 6-6):

Figure 6-6. Latin.

I especially love this groove. It's not only a lot of fun to play and musically hip, but can also be assimilated fairly intuitively into the palettes of most bass players. It *feels* right, and unlike some other grooves in Latin music, it's a little more easily learned without necessitating weeks, months, or years of hard study!

Harmonically, the typical tumbao bass line uses the root and the fifth almost exclusively. The harmonic twist is that the rhythm generally dictates that chord changes are *anticipated* (or rhythmically pushed) to occur immediately before beat 1. Let me explain.

The tumbao bass figure is a complimentary rhythmic pattern to the *clave* (the heartbeat of Afro-Cuban music). For more information on clave, see the "Suggested Resources" section. The tumbao rhythm is based upon playing on the *and* of beat 2 and on beat 4—in cut time, so the measures are going by twice as fast.

As a quick aside—although it wouldn't usually be written this way—you might find it easier to assimilate the basic part by counting it in noncut time: the rhythmic placement would then be the fourth sixteenth note of beat 1 ("1-e-and-**a**") and the *and* of beat 2, then repeating that figure again over beats 3 and 4 ("3-e-and-**a**" and the *and* of beat 4).

A normal convention of this groove is to play the fifth of the upcoming chord on the *and* of beat 2 immediately preceding the chord change (back in cut-time, of course!) and the root of the upcoming chord on beat 4. You'll see this demonstrated throughout the written example. Consequently, the tumbao doesn't usually hit beat 1 except at the beginning of the song; the rest of the tune, your note is sustained right through the downbeat of the new bar. With a bit of practice and thinking ahead as you're playing through a tune, this chord anticipation starts feeling natural.

As with many musical styles, it is extremely valuable to listen to the masters and glean from them. This is particularly important for Latin music, largely due to the organic nature of the time; experienced Latin musicians infuse a somewhat difficult-to-quantify but incredibly musical pushing and pulling of the time—versus metronomically precise subdivision (as in the programmed example here!) Any of you who've programmed and quantized a Latin percussion groove can attest to this. Authenticity of the feel is dependent upon this elasticity.

Sonically, this type of bass line usually benefits from a warm tone that emulates an upright bass. For this reason, experienced bassists will typically move up the neck to keep playing the groove on the heavier strings rather than ascending to the higher, lighter-gauge strings.

Reggae

Every bassist can benefit from having a fundamental grasp of the reggae style. Here's a reggae-inspired version of the chord progression (Figure 6-7):

Figure 6-7. Reggae.

Even if your typical playing situation doesn't involve a proliferation of dreadlocks and guitar-chords-on-every-upbeat, it's a fun and interesting genre that can be applied in a multitude of settings.

I like to subtly drop reggae-inspired bass lines into tunes that are decidedly nonreggae— ballads or middle-of-the-road pop, for instance—and it often introduces a bit of musical freshness. Most folks who hear these lines in context wouldn't associate them with that genre; the lines simply infuse sparseness and rhythmic variation that nicely contrast with the rest of the tune.

To me, that is one of the biggest reasons to pursue having a variety of styles in your musical vocabulary: it allows you to have a diverse spectrum of colors that can be applied to the musical canvas. These genres can be applied as overtly or as subtly as musical sensitivity dictates in the particular setting.

It should be noted that the written example is for a shuffled reggae groove, so the sixteenth notes should be shuffled as reflected in Figure 6-8.

Figure 6-8. Shuffled sixteenth notes.

As with many other genres, it's common to see examples of both straight and shuffle feels in the reggae style. Make sure to be aware of which one you're playing at a given time, so that you can avoid unintentional "groovicide."

This type of groove is characterized by a very laid-back rhythmic approach. If you rush this type of line, phrasing it on top, it gives it an urgency that lacks authenticity. Don't be afraid to phrase your part in a very relaxed and lazy manner—versus emulating your sequencer's "100 percent quantize" function.

I employ a different right-hand technique when playing reggae lines to help achieve the requisite warm, staccato, muted tone. It involves plucking the strings with the fleshy part of the thumb while dampening them with the palm near the bridge saddles. If you experiment with how close to the bridge saddles you rest your palm—as well as how much pressure you apply to the strings—you'll discover a really broad range of timbres.

Rhythmically, you're probably already aware that a traditional reggae bass line will frequently not play on beat 1. In this example, I employed this rhythmic convention in bars 1, 4, 5, and 7; the remainder of the time, I was pretty much answering the phrase of the previous measure. This rhythmic approach can really give an arrangement some openness and room to breathe.

Sonically, this style is characterized by a warm, thudlike tone. Most of this is controlled by technique, but if necessary, roll off your treble knob to minimize fret noise and the "zing" of fresh roundwound strings.

Rock

Here is one of countless possible rock approaches to the tune (Figure 6-9):

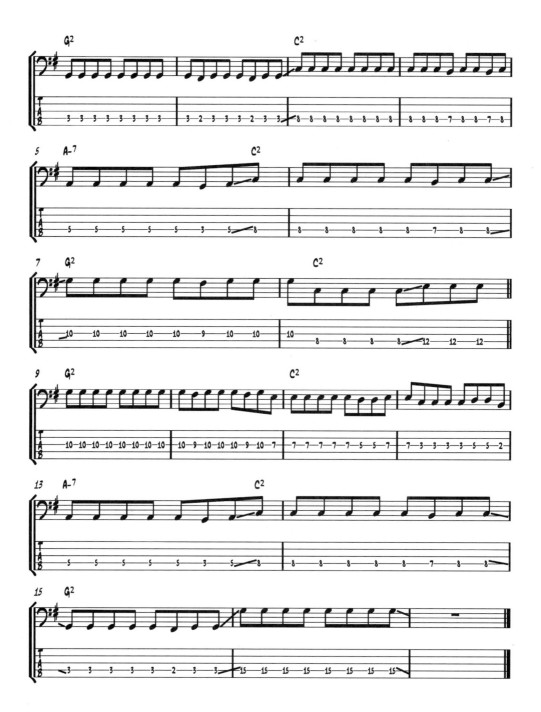

Figure 6-9. Rock.

When addressing a music that spans the range from Metallica to the Beatles and beyond, it's difficult to get too definitive about particular idioms. I'll be describing general characteristics that apply broadly to rock music, while perhaps thinking along the lines of the approach typically associated with bands such as U2 and Coldplay that has become so ubiquitous.

The rock style is fundamentally about energy, edge, and attitude. Sliding into notes in the upper register—especially on the lower, heavier strings—is a common phrasing idiom in a driving rock feel, and sounds huge in the proper context. A riff-oriented approach can also be effective in rock, perhaps to a greater extent than in most other styles.

Rhythmically, rock is usually based around an eighth-note subdivision feel. Phrasing varies, but generally is a bit on top of the beat for driving, up-tempo tunes while laying back for slower tunes or ballads.

Harmonically, it's usually fairly diatonic without a lot of "pretty" chords (major 7th and so on). Pentatonic scales are commonly employed. It's uncommon to hear much *chromaticism* in rock music. Much of the current rock approach also employs tension by substituting "2" chords—D2, F2, and so on, which comprise the root, second, and fifth only—for major chords. So it stands to reason that ninths can frequently be a good choice for embellishments. Heavier or edgier rock commonly uses flatted-ninths or flatted-fifths for tension as well. However, most mainstream examples employ fairly "inside," diatonic harmony.

Sonically, rock tone generally has a degree of drive or edge accomplished through technique and/or compression, overdrive, and so on. This topic could easily fill a chapter or two, but suffice it to say that the context will largely dictate the preferred approach and tone. If the bass is to be a warm, thick, and unobtrusive glue between the drums and walls of guitar and keyboard tracks, it's usually preferable to play conservatively—limiting excessive fret noise and clack—to allow the tone to be heavily compressed by a recording or live sound engineer without problematic loud transients. If the music is more raw and aggressive, digging in hard with a pick—with the accompanying fret and string noises—can be just the desired statement. Even in the latter scenario, though, a fair amount of compression would very commonly be employed. Consequently, a relatively even dynamic level can help your part sit in the mix more easily.

Hybrid

Combining elements of various styles into one groove can render some of the most interesting bass lines. Sure, there are definitely times when the musical context calls for strict adherence to the idioms of the style—your bandmates might experience some heartburn if they hear you throwing disco licks into that country tune—but there are other occasions when creative application from the spectrum of genres can be incredibly hip.

Anyone who has enjoyed the music of Bela Fleck and the Flecktones can attest to this: they seamlessly incorporate elements of bluegrass, jazz, funk, rock, rap, and countless other styles. It's amazing and extremely creative stuff.

Here's a groove that incorporates a number of different elements from the styles we've already discussed (Figure 6-10):

Figure 6-10. Hybrid.

You'll find walk-ups from the country style, passing tones from jazz, some of the ghost-note ideas from the funk feel, and an overall Latin-inspired rhythmic approach.

Departing from the chord progression, here's a fun acid-jazz vamp in B♭ that incorporates idioms from jazz, funk, Latin, and even a bit of hip-hop in the drums (Figure 6-11). The sixteenth notes are shuffled (see Figure 6-8).

Figure 6-11. Hybrid vamp.

And while you're having fun with it, here's a riff-oriented groove (Figure 6-12) that combines rock and funk, with even a dash of reggae implied in the drum fill. In an ensemble, a guitar would likely double parts of this bass line.

Another shuffled-sixteenth groove for you; the sky's the limit—you take it from here!

Figure 6-12. Hybrid riff.

Let's Grab Coffee:
Real-World Groove Lesson

A number of years ago, I went through an extremely challenging experience that proved to be a true test of the real-world applicability of many of the concepts in this book. Despite being one of the more trying things I've gone through as a musician, it also served to renew my awareness and appreciation for some fundamental dynamics of effective rhythm sections. It is absolutely not my intention to disparage anyone or rant through the following story; rather, my hope is that you might glean some insight and be equipped should you find yourself in a similar situation.

I've spent much time over the years working with students to help develop their ability to function in any rhythm section—and, more specifically, be effective bassists with any given drummer. I believe that this ability to be able to play well with whoever happens to be sitting behind the drum kit is one of the most critical for any working bassist to possess. In my own experience, this ability has been one of the primary reasons my phone keeps ringing—much more so than any chops, the right gear, or cool attire!

So now on to my challenging episode. I found myself playing with a drummer—we'll call him Jeff—with whom I had a casual friendship but no familiarity with his playing. I did know that he had played with some fairly high-profile artists and was a technically proficient, capable drummer. However, several bars into the first tune, it became immediately apparent to me that there was a major problem. I was discovering that Jeff and I had divergent and conflicting rhythmic vocabularies—basically, profoundly different ideas of beat placement for purposes of grooving. By the fourth bar of the tune, I was watching and intently listening to his kick drum, trying to discern the rhythmic pattern being played. By the sixteenth bar, I concluded that the kick-drum pattern was in a more-or-less constant state of flux. By the thirty-second bar, I was utterly exasperated from my fruitless efforts to play something cohesive with Jeff. By the end of the song, I was scratching my head in bewilderment at what I had just experienced: playing an entire tune—albeit our first run-through of the song—with a highly experienced drummer and having absolutely no sense that we'd functioned as a *rhythm section*. In every way, it was really just a drummer and a bassist playing at the same time—but definitely not serving as any sort of musical foundation for the rest of the band. We played through several other tunes, all of which confirmed that the first tune wasn't a fluke!

To be candid, this experience was really unsettling. Having played with dozens of different drummers at every level of ability over the years, I've always derived a certain satisfaction from being able to listen to a particular drummer's beat placement and rhythmic patterns, adapt my playing, and groove along with him or her. Yet I was now finding myself stumped, frankly.

After much analysis of the situation, I concluded that the primary source of our problems was the absence of two of the fundamental and critical factors common to most effective impromptu—or thrown together for a particular gig—rhythm sections.

Play a Part...Remember?

I covered this in the last "Let's Grab Coffee" segment, but here it is illuminated in an actual playing situation. The importance of playing a consistent, relatively easily recognized pattern can't be overemphasized.

Most groove-oriented music employs this concept of repetition, or establishing a motif, which gradually and progressively introduces variations to the original repetitive motif as the song develops. Constant variation, especially rhythmically, is ineffective in most musical contexts, is usually a major contributor to the musical arrangement being perceived as busy, and is frequently countergroove in its effect. The majority of the time I spent playing through the tunes with Jeff involved trying to adapt my bass line to a constantly changing kick-drum pattern. This ties into the second factor.

Simplify

There are certainly a number of notable rhythm sections that play complex and ever-evolving patterns and are still able to maintain a sense of cohesion. This is usually the product of a great deal of familiarity between the rhythm section players after spending many years working together.

On the other hand, when you find yourself in an ensemble with a musician with whom you have no previous playing experience or familiarity with that player's vocabulary—as is frequently the case in many worship environments—the bottom line is *simplify*. Particularly if you and the drummer find yourselves playing incompatible parts early in a tune, it is so essential that both players activate their most acute listening skills and immediately edit their own parts to a simple motif. It is not enough for one or both players to detect that something isn't quite right yet continue to barrel through the tune, making no adjustment to help remedy the situation. When you and the drummer simplify your parts, it's akin to helping each other climb from a turbulent sea into a lifeboat. Once you're making a compatible statement together and the rhythmic foundation is established, then gradual variations from that motif can be explored.

Postlude

The next time you find yourself in a situation similar to the one I've described, I encourage you to evaluate whether either—or both—of these factors is at the heart of the issue. I believe that you and the drummer will find resolution through a combination of good and responsive listening, a servant's attitude toward the ensemble and each other, flexibility, reasonable technique, and much prayer!

7

Chart Fundamentals

Speaking from experience, I know how challenging it can be to encounter any form of written music when you don't have a music-reading background. Our pianist colleagues were reading the proverbial mouse-droppings-scattered-densely-on-manuscript-paper—pardon the visual—years before most of us were locked in our bedrooms learning tunes by ear.

I'd been playing for almost 12 years when I went back and taught myself how to read. It took some work, but I can honestly say that it was worth every bit of effort. The merits of being able to read go on and on: you don't need to memorize every tune in the repertoire, you can capably sub in other groups or situations, you are eligible for a broad range of recording and performance opportunities not available to nonreaders, most music educational resources require reading, and so on. It's an enormously valuable skill to bring to the gig.

The good news is that there aren't any real secrets. It's just a matter of putting in the time on a consistent basis. It's amazing how quickly it comes together.

Part 1

I'll be exploring a chart and hopefully demystifying it for those of you intimidated by anything resembling written music. Please bear in mind that this won't be a comprehensive music-reading course; rather, I'll cover some of the essentials to get you up and running. Let's dive in.

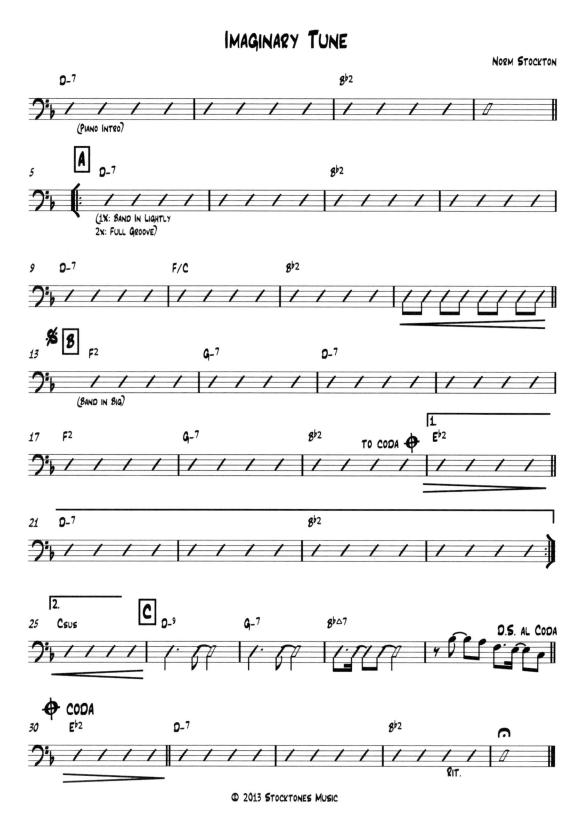

Figure 7-1. "Imaginary Tune" rhythm chart.

This chart of "Imaginary Tune" (it's just that; the song isn't real but the chart is!) is what is commonly referred to as a *rhythm chart* and is far and away my favorite to see on my music stand. It clearly reflects the essentials—tempo, time signature, key, chords, sections, basic dynamics, road map, any hits or moments where certain rhythms are prescribed—and any specific lines that the bass should play. It's much more common to see charts like this versus those where the bass line is notated in its entirety. A rhythm chart gives the players freedom to come up with their own grooves and parts in the style that the bandleader or ensemble chooses. Only the critical elements are actually specified or notated—see bars 12 and 26–29.

Let's look at a couple of basics. The bass clef on the staff lets you know that you don't need to transpose any written notes you encounter from treble clef—always good to know! The small symbol resembling a *b* next to the bass clef, a flat symbol, is on the staff line representing the note B—indicating that all Bs encountered should be flatted or lowered by one fret or half step. A quick trip down "music-theory Memory Lane" should bring to mind that this would be consistent with F major—or its relative minor, D. Hence, the key of this piece is D minor—no *Spinal Tap* jokes, please!

You'll notice that there are four slashes per measure, each representing a quarter note. Four beats per bar identifies the time signature as 4/4. The top staff reflects two bars of Dm7 (again, the minus sign is a common convention for referring to "minor," as is a small triangle for indicating "major") and two bars of Bb2.

Bar 4—the last measure of the top staff—shows a diamond. That indicates that any instruments playing should hit a whole note and hold it for the full four beats. A quick glance at the text below bar 1 reveals that the pianist is the only player involved at the moment—so in a real-world application, you'd just listen to see if it's possible for a pianist to actually play a whole note without throwing in some lavish arpeggio!

Part 2

Having listened to the tickling of ivories during those first four measures, you'll come in lightly on bar five—where the text specifies that the first time through, the band should come in at a soft dynamic level.

Note the *rehearsal mark*: that large A at bar 5. It gives a clear location or section reference that's readily visible, even when quickly glancing over from another sheet of a tune. Rehearsal marks are usually placed at the beginning of new song sections—for instance, the beginning of the verse, chorus, bridge, outro, and so on.

You'll also notice that there's a *start repeat* sign: the doubled bar lines with colon symbol to the right. That symbol indicates that at a certain point, you'll be jumping back to this point in the tune. Just make a quick mental note for now.

As mentioned earlier, each measure has four slashes—representing quarter notes. If the song was in a different time signature—say, 3/4—there would only be three slashes per bar. The slashes simply mean that the arranger or composer isn't specifying or dictating a specific part to play—in which case the line would have been written in standard notation—rather, the musicians may spontaneously conceptualize and perform their own parts as they freely interpret the tune in whatever musical style the band chooses.

Anyway, once in at bar 5, you would just play along and follow the chord changes, keeping things at a fairly low level dynamically.

At bar 12, there is an eighth-note build-up into the chorus or B-section, indicated by the *crescendo* hairpin below the staff. That would have you gradually increasing the dynamic level over the course of that measure ("one-and-two-and-three-and-four-and").

You can see the second rehearsal mark (B) at bar 13, the beginning of what is presumably the chorus section. There's also text below the staff that specifies "Band in Big"—so you're apparently rocking at this point. Lastly, there's a symbol that resembles an S with a diagonal line through it and two dots: that's a DS sign—for *dal segno*, which means "from the sign." Make another quick mental note; I'll explain this when you're directed to jump back to this bar at some point later in the tune.

You're dynamically big as you blast your way through the chorus. At the end of bar 19, it specifies "to Coda"—with accompanying bulls-eye symbol. Ignore it on your first time through this section, but make a third mental note! That instruction will be applicable later in the tune.

At bar 20, you kick into the first ending—the second ending is at bar 25, by the way—while also dropping the dynamic level back down in response to the diminuendo hairpin below bar 20, presumably to get ready for the second verse.

You may notice that bars 21–24 look a lot like the first four bars of the tune. It's essentially a re-intro, but this time with the full band playing—at a softer dynamic level following bar 20.

At the end of bar 24, you'll notice an *end repeat* sign—again the doubled bar lines, but this time the colon symbol is to the left. This instructs you to play through bar 24, then jump back and play from the preceding start repeat sign at bar 5 by rehearsal mark A. See how that works?

So now you're on your second time through the A-section. The text below bar 5 indicates that you should be playing a full groove this time—instead of the "band in lightly" approach from the first pass, which probably involved a lot of tied whole notes, cymbal tinkles, and so on.

Everything's pretty much the same through the verse and chorus (B-section), except that both sections are probably dynamically bigger this time. It makes sense; you've already played through the full tune once, so you should probably lay in a bit more now that the tune is established.

As you approach bar 19, you again notice the "to Coda" comment—but it still doesn't apply! *"Deep breath. Paaaaaatience."*

This time, you'll play through bar 19 and jump right to bar 25—the second ending, as you've already played the first ending. Bar 25 shows another crescendo, so build into the next section of the tune—indicated by rehearsal mark C, which looks to be the bridge.

Part 3

Notice that the arranger or composer now is specifying the rhythms to play. These are simple, very common phrases that should be part of your memorized vocabulary of rhythms; they shouldn't require you to stop and count. There are only so many permutations of sixteenth-note rhythms—most rhythm charts won't reference thirty-second notes—so musicians can readily acquire the rhythmic sight-reading skills with regular practice.

Getting back to the chart, you'll play through the rhythms reflected in bars 26–28 of the C-section before playing the written line in bar 29. This is very common for a rhythm chart: the composer or arranger only notates the parts where it's important to play a specific line—possibly a unison line with some of the other instruments. You'll notice that bar 29 contains the only actual notation on this chart.

When you're new to reading, I encourage you to go straight to any notated lines as soon as you're handed the chart. You can then wrap your head around it without the pressure of sight-reading it on the spot and at tempo.

As you're playing through the written line in bar 29, notice the text above the staff—"D.S. al Coda." Here's where you circle back to those three mental notes you made!

"D.S. al Coda" is directing the musician to jump back to the DS sign and play from there until directed to the coda—at which point you jump to the coda.

So that means that you'd go from the end of bar 29, back to the DS at bar 13, play through the B-section until the end of bar 19, then jump down to bar 30—the coda—to finish the tune. Or to put it in musical terms: go from the bridge back to a final chorus, then play an outro section to end the song.

Bar 30 has a diminuendo—the term *decrescendo* is often used interchangeably—directing you to bring the dynamic level back down for a soft conclusion to the tune.

The text below bar 33 ("rit.") indicates that the guitarist should play a Lee Ritenour lick at this point. Just kidding. Sorry. Actually, it stands for *ritardando*, more commonly referred to as a *ritard*, which is a direction to slow down the tempo.

That nicely sets up the final whole note in the last bar of the tune. The symbol above the diamond is a *fermata* sign, which generally directs a musical pause, but which is frequently used in this manner to indicate that the note should "swell": quickly dynamically build then drop off.

There you have it! Really not that tough, was it? It's just a matter of getting familiar with the symbols and conventions of written music. With just a rudimentary grasp of chart reading, an ensemble on the very first run-through could perform a song like this "Imaginary Tune" convincingly. That's powerful stuff!

Other Common Chart Sightings

- *DC*, or *da capo*, which simply means go back to the beginning of the tune.
- *al fine*—pronounced "al fee-neh" (vs. "all fine!")—which means "end."

So a note indicating "DC al Fine" means "Go back to the beginning, and play through to the end." "DS al Fine" would mean "Go back to the DS sign and play through to the end."

Lastly, some of you classically trained folks are wondering why this chart doesn't reflect dynamic notations such as *p*, *mp*, *f*, and so on. It's actually not uncommon to see them on a chart in a pop or nonclassical setting; however, for many rhythm charts, the intent is to leave most of that to the discretion of the musicians in the moment. That allows greater freedom to interpret the tune differently from night to night.

Tips

1. When you get to the gig, scan and read through anything noteworthy or potentially challenging, including any written lines or rhythmic hits, unfamiliar time signatures, exceptionally fast or slow tempos, passages where the chart indicates a bass solo, and so on.

2. See if the road maps are clear or if there are chart errors—for example, "DS al Coda" marks with no apparent DS signs. Get clarification from the musical director prior to downbeat if possible.

3. Take a highlighter and make the charts exceedingly clear. If I have the time, I will frequently highlight enty points, repeats, DS signs, codas, any important dynamic or articulation directions, written passages or rhythmic hits, sections where the bass is to lay out, and so on. For long or confusing charts, I've sometimes even drawn arrows pointing toward a DS sign halfway down the preceding page, for instance—anything to keep from having to search for directions! Those all help ensure success when the time comes to play down the tune.

4. Most importantly, the best way to develop your reading is by reading. Read often; consistency is the key!

8

The Slap Technique

Ever since bassist Larry Graham first applied thumb to electric bass string in the late 1960s, in an effort to provide rhythmic support when his mom's trio lost their drummer, the bass world has never been the same. The "slap and pop" technique became and remains very popular among bassists in a broad variety of musical styles. In the hands of a tasteful player, the slap technique can be extremely effective for injecting punch and rhythmic syncopation—as well as a bit of attitude. However, it can also be quite *un*musical and intrusive when applied without discernment and sensitivity to the musical context.

As this book is geared toward the worship musician, let me quickly take a moment to preface:

- If your church's musical style isn't conducive to incorporating slap playing in the worship set, please don't. There are few things more painful than hearing someone trying to force slap into music that clearly doesn't call for it. Besides, remember that musical styles are cyclical; be patient and your church's music may be slap friendly soon!
- That said, I think it's a musically valuable and expressive technique to have in your repertoire—whether for Sunday mornings or for other musical settings— and I wholeheartedly encourage you to get it into your musical bag.

The Mechanics

I'll start by examining the fundamental technique before delving into the practical applications. By the way, many of these exercises cover the range of a five-string bass but are easily adapted; feel free to tweak as needed should you run out of strings or have extras!

Part 1

The basic technique involves percussively bouncing your thumb off the string at the end of the fingerboard. Fresh roundwound strings are an essential part of the tone. The trick is to not excessively tense up your thumb; while you don't want it flopping loosely, keeping it relaxed is definitely helpful for facilitating the technique. Additionally, experiment to determine the *least* amount of force necessary to strike the string and still achieve the desired timbre. If your thumb's range of motion—from maximum *recoil* to the point at which it strikes the string—exceeds approximately 7–8 inches, then you're probably pulling your striking hand up too far, which will usually result in lots of unintentional contact with adjacent strings and present a muting nightmare. String-skipping exercises will also help develop accuracy with your thumb, which is critical for clean slapping. When slapping the higher strings—the D and G—try to make the trajectory of your thumb more *across* the string than straight down. This will help those lighter strings match the output of the heavier strings.

Exercises 1A and 1B in Figure 8-1 develop the fundamental slap motion. Take your time and be patient; it might take a few sessions to assimilate if you're new to this. Be sure to review the preceding and ensure that you're achieving the desired tone with the least amount of striking force.

Figure 8-1. Slap Exercise 1.

Exercise 2 introduces some string skipping. Sticking with open strings for these exercises allows you to focus exclusively on your thumb.

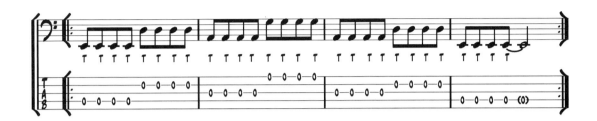

Figure 8-2. Slap Exercise 2.

It's **critically** important to ensure that you warm up your hands and forearms prior to spending much time working on this technique; you can cause serious damage to your tendons by neglecting this advice (see the "Tips for the Woodshed" chapter for warm-ups)!

The response to the slap is the pop, which is achieved by pulling up and percussively releasing—usually with the index finger—one of the higher strings immediately after the slap. So the full technique involves slapping a note (normally on one of the lower strings as the striking hand descends) and then popping a note (normally on one of the higher strings as the striking hand ascends). The resulting pendulum motion is helpful for keeping rhythmic solidity.

Exercises 3A and 3B introduce the slap and pop. Simple octaves are a good way to get your fretting hand involved.

Figure 8-3. Slap Exercise 3.

Once you're comfortable with the basic motion, turn on the metronome and work on developing rhythmic accuracy. Few techniques emphasize time inconsistencies as much as slapping! Additionally, make an effort to keep the dynamic range, or relative loudness, reasonably consistent between your slaps and pops.

Part 2

I hope you're starting to acclimate to the basic mechanics of the slap motion! If you're finding it a bit challenging, no worries: it will definitely come together with consistent repetition.

Exercise 4 adds a few more variables to Exercise 3B (Figure 8-3) from last time. You'll notice that beats 2 and 4 are played staccato: tightly, with minimal note duration. Developing the ability to control note duration while slapping will be valuable when it comes time to actually make music.

Figure 8-4. Slap Exercise 4.

Exercise 5 has the staccato note on beat 1. Let the other notes ring full value. It also adds a bit of funkiness with the flatted-seventh motion on beat 3. As before, once you've got the exercise under your fingers, practice it to a metronome to ensure rhythmic accuracy.

Figure 8-5. Slap Exercise 5.

In Exercise 6, play bars 1 and 3 staccato, then legato (letting the notes ring full value) in bars 2 and 4.

Figure 8-6. Slap Exercise 6.

Exercise 7 introduces a couple of new elements. The muted slap on the *and* of beat 1 is accomplished by slapping in the normal manner, but while muting the string with the fretting hand—the finger lightly resting on the string but not fretting the note. This produces a ghost note, which is a staple of the slap vocabulary. You'll also see a hammer-on on beats 2 and 4 of each bar. After popping the first note, fret the second note with another finger on your fretting hand. You'll probably recognize this as a familiar sound; it's used all the time in slapping.

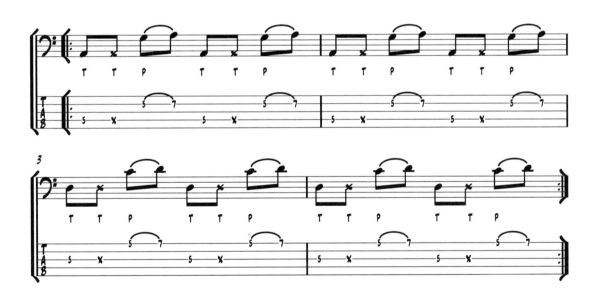

Figure 8-7. Slap Exercise 7.

Exercise 8 incorporates the muted slap and that pop/hammer-on combination, while also adding a hammer-on to the slapped note on the *and* of beat two.

Figure 8-8. Slap Exercise 8.

Part 3

Pretty fun, right? Continuing on, the exercises this time are a natural progression from the material I've covered so far.

As always, make sure to properly warm up before woodshedding, and take frequent breaks to ensure that you don't give yourself tendinitis—seriously!

Exercise 9 involves many of the elements you've already practiced—ghost notes, octave patterns, string skipping—while also introducing sixteenth notes to the palette. Don't be intimidated by the figure occurring on beat 3: it's simply the same familiar octave pattern but played twice as fast. If necessary, start out playing as slowly as you need, then gradually work up the tempo as it gets comfortable.

Figure 8-9. Slap Exercise 9.

Focus on accuracy when going back and forth between A and D—the transition occurs between the first two measures and the latter two—ensuring that your thumb is only striking the intended string.

Exercise 10 is an abbreviated version of the previous exercise but also incorporates a staccato note on the *and* of beat 1, as well as slurs and hammers.

Figure 8-10. Slap Exercise 10.

Exercise 11 mixes things up just a bit but should come together quickly. Note the vibrato on beat 1. Try to make it overt enough that there's a little attitude on those notes; think synth bass. I'd recommend more of an up-and-down versus side-to-side vibrato technique to accomplish the desired effect.

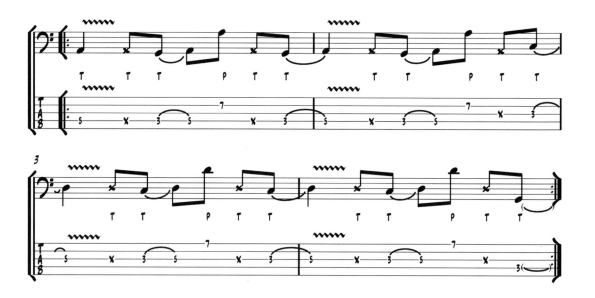

Figure 8-11. Slap Exercise 11.

Once you have the exercises under your fingers, play along with a metronome—a tempo of 90 to 100 bpm works well for these—and make them groove!

Part 4

Let's kick it up another notch. Again, don't forget to warm up before working on these for any length of time, and take periodic breathers to stretch and rest your hands/arms.

Exercise 12 introduces slapping and popping on the same string, as well as further reinforces accuracy by incorporating string skipping.

Figure 8-12. Slap Exercise 12.

I find it helpful to integrate both the thumb slap and index finger positioning—for the proceeding pop—into one motion or consolidated move. That way, the pop simply involves the upward motion to pluck the string percussively. Try to keep the dynamic level between the slaps and pops fairly consistent, and work on rhythmic accuracy.

Exercise 13 involves thumb slaps exclusively, with lots of string skipping. I encourage you to initially play this as slowly as necessary to ensure accuracy—that you're not inadvertently hitting adjacent strings—and then gradually work the tempo up to speed.

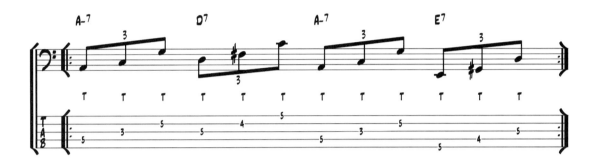

Figure 8-13. Slap Exercise 13.

Exercise 14 mixes things up just a bit. Instead of ascending through each figure, you're now slapping the root, popping the seventh, and slapping the third. Additionally, the exercise is to be played staccato in the first bar and legato—not overlapping, but no *air* between the notes—in the second bar. This note duration is entirely a function of your fretting hand.

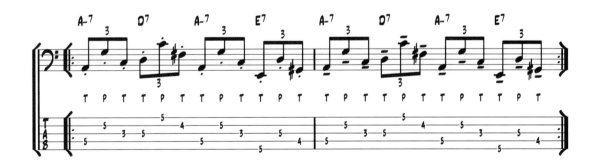

Figure 8-14. Slap Exercise 14.

Exercise 15 introduces another slap idiom in the form of the left-hand slap. This is accomplished by percussively slapping your flatted fretting-hand fingers against the fingerboard. It will take a bit of practice to achieve the desired "thump"—versus hammering and actually fretting the strings so that they generate pitched notes. The objective of this type of left-hand slap is to create a ghost note. After you get the basic motion together, practice to get the relative loudness of the left-hand slap fairly even with the slapped note.

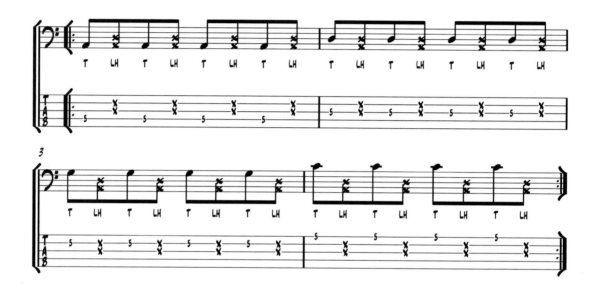

Figure 8-15. Slap Exercise 15.

Exercise 16 combines both fretted and muted slaps, left-hand slaps, pops, and hammers.

Figure 8-16. Slap Exercise 16.

Congratulations on your progress so far! We'll now start delving into some advanced slapping.

Part 5

Exercise 17 incorporates the left-hand slap that I covered last time, as well as hammers, ghost notes, string skipping, and slaps and pops on the same string. Play it slowly until you get it under your fingers, and then work it up to tempo with a metronome.

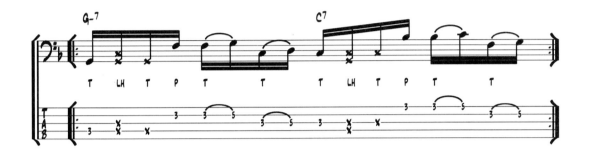

Figure 8-17. Slap Exercise 17.

Exercise 18 has a similar feel, but you'll notice that the left-hand slap is now a hammer. This is accomplished by simply fretting the note percussively with your fretting fingers instead of playing a muted thump. This exercise also introduces some funk idioms by departing from the octave patterns so prevalent in slap playing.

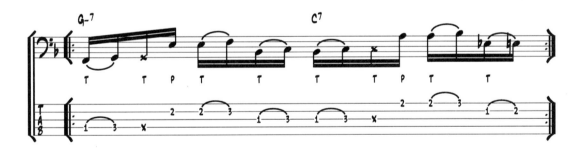

Figure 8-18. Slap Exercise 18.

Exercise 19 introduces *double-thumbing*, the popular approach employed so effectively by players like Victor Wooten. The basic mechanics of the technique involve a simple down-and-up motion with the thumb, similar to using a pick. If you're new to double-thumbing, you will likely find it pretty uncomfortable at first; roundwound strings wearing away the soft and uncalloused area on the top of the thumb takes some getting used to! Don't get discouraged. It comes together pretty quickly with consistent practice.

Figure 8-19. Slap Exercise 19.

My recommendation for those of you just starting out with double-thumbing is to begin by simply working on the down-and-up motion on a single string—start with the highest string, then gradually work your way to the E or B strings—until it starts feeling less weird. You can then dive into the exercise, which is simply a D major scale. Playing scales helps to develop accuracy with the thumb. Strive to only strike the intended string and for consistency in tone between strings.

As always, once you have the exercises under your fingers, play along with a metronome and focus on rhythmic accuracy.

Part 6

I'd like to take a final look at the mechanics of slapping before getting into its practical usage in the next part.

Both exercises utilize the double-thumb technique—hopefully, the basic motion is starting to feel a little less uncomfortable by now! If not, don't worry; with consistent repetition, it will come together.

Exercise 20 reprises the D major scale from before, but now with the addition of a single pop—normally with the index finger of the plucking hand.

The key is to combine the thumb slap with getting your index finger into popping position so that those two elements become a single fluid motion. Once you get a basic feel

Figure 8-20. Slap Exercise 20.

for it, turn on the metronome and work on rhythmic and dynamic consistency—ensuring that the triplets are rhythmically even and that the loudness of the thumb slap, thumb upstroke, and pop are all in the same ballpark.

Are you hanging in there? Again, take your time and be patient with yourself; this is probably an entirely new way of playing for many of you.

Once you have that under your fingers, it's not that difficult to add a second pop. Exercise 21 involves a down- and upstroke with the thumb, a pop with the index finger ("i"), and another pop with the middle finger ("m"). The same principle from earlier applies here: get your index and middle fingers into place at the same time that the thumb slap occurs.

To introduce some string skipping, this exercise involves playing that D major scale in staggered thirds and alternating between ascending and descending with every other pair. That's much harder to describe than it is in reality; check out Figure 8-21 and you'll see

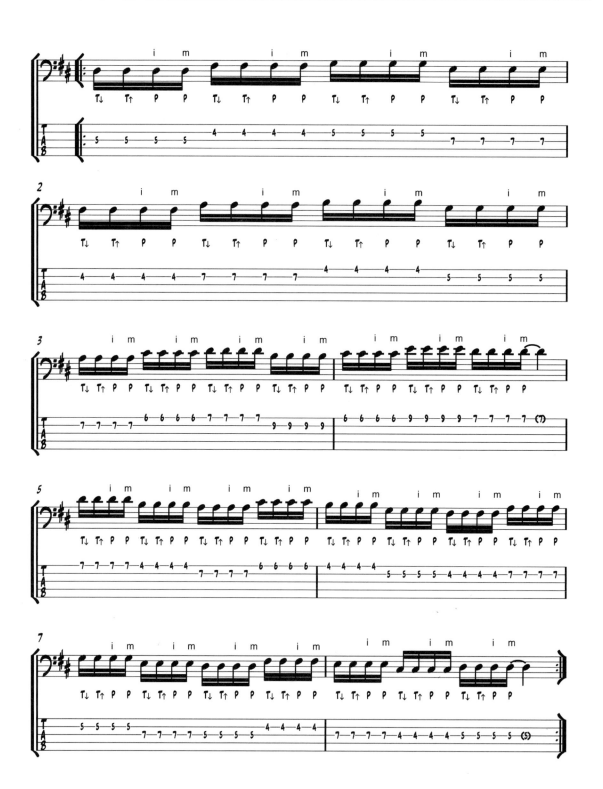

Figure 8-21. Slap Exercise 21.

what I mean! Play it as slowly as necessary to maintain accuracy, and ensure that you're only hitting the desired strings with your plucking hand.

Have fun, and get ready for some musical application!

Practical Application

Congratulations on successfully making it through the "basic mechanics" phase of developing your slap technique; now for the fun stuff! Let's explore some actual musical applications of slapping.

Part 1

Exercise 22 is an example of the subtle incorporation of the slap technique in an R&B ballad.

You can see that only bars 3, 5, and 7 contain any significant slapping, whereas the remainder of the groove is played with a conventional fingerstyle approach. The trick is to ensure that the dynamic level is generally consistent between the fingerstyle and slapped or

Figure 8-22. Slap Exercise 22 (R&B ballad).

popped notes—in other words, that the slapped or popped notes don't obliterate listeners seated within the first three rows of the venue while the fingerstyle notes remain barely audible! Practice alternating between fingerstyle and slapping while maintaining the same apparent loudness between the two.

Exercise 23 is a contemporary/urban Gospel shuffled groove that employs the slap technique more predominantly.

Notice the liberal use of space; the adage about what is *not* played being just as important as what *is* played is most assuredly true. It's relatively easy to play a steady stream

Figure 8-23. Slap Exercise 23 (Gospel groove).

of sixteenth notes using the slap technique, but it's considerably more musical to only play what is necessary and leave some air in the bass line.

Part 2

While the upcoming bass lines will increase in complexity a bit, the fundamentals of the technique remain the same. Feel free to slow down the tempo in the provided examples as much as necessary to execute them accurately—and then gradually increase the pace. As always, let these examples serve as a springboard for your own original bass grooves.

Exercise 24 is a shuffled funk groove at approximately 92 bpm that incorporates basic slapping with a few dashes of spice. It actually looks a bit more complicated than it sounds, as I made an effort to accurately transcribe the phrasing. Be overt with the vibrato; this is not the context for subtlety!

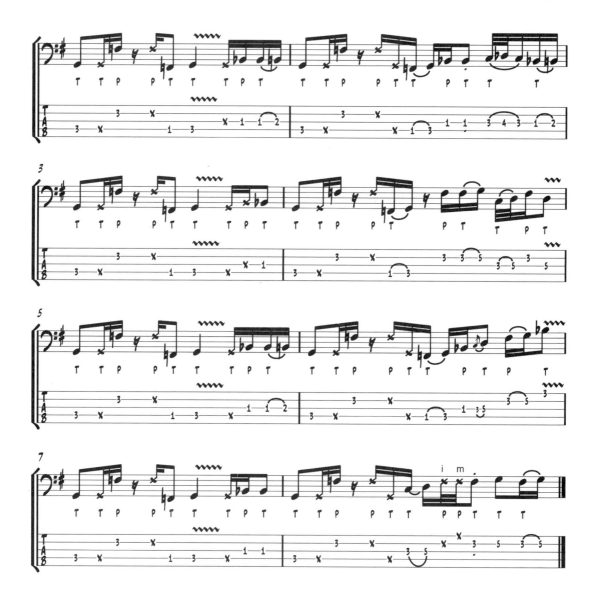

Figure 8-24. Slap Exercise 24 (funk shuffle).

Other points of note: you'll see several examples of slapping and popping on the same string; if this feels awkward, spend some time focusing on that specific element. Also, in the final bar, you'll notice a *double pop* immediately following beat 3. This is accomplished by popping the muted D and G strings—with the index and middle fingers, respectively—in rapid succession, with the motion generally limited to a twist of the wrist. With a bit of practice, it comes together.

Exercise 25 is an excerpt from a tune entitled "A Tender NAMM Moment," from my *Pondering the Sushi* CD, and reflects the basic A-section motif. The tempo is approximately 120 bpm, and the time signature can be thought of as 4/4, with an underlying triplet subdivision, or as 12/8. You'll notice that the bass line in bars 1 through 4 is essentially repeated in bars 5 through 8, with variations occurring in bars 2 and 6.

Figure 8-25. Slap Exercise 25 (groove from "A Tender NAMM Moment").

Slapwise, it again employs a lot of standard slap technique with a couple of tweaks. The first of these is the popped *double-stops* (two-note chords) occurring at the end of bars 1, 3, 5, and 7, and the beginning of bars 2, 4, 6, and 8. Those are played by popping the D and G strings in a similar manner to the double-pop technique covered earlier, but playing the notes simultaneously—versus the two thirty-second notes from Exercise 24—and employing actual fretted notes versus muted ghost notes. The end of bar 2 contains the aforementioned double-popped thirty-second-note lick found in the last bar of Exercise 24. Bar 6 incorporates the double-thumb/double-pop lick I covered back in "The Mechanics" section, part 6. This sort of lick is most effective when employed sparingly; resist the temptation to liberally insert such lines throughout your grooves, as they can tend to make things sound cluttered in a hurry. As with using spices when preparing a meal, they're most enjoyable when carefully incorporated with tasteful restraint!

Part 3

I'll be pulling out all the stops in this final slap lesson and looking at a bass part that incorporates a number of fairly advanced applications of the technique: double-thumbing, double-popping, and rapid-fire thirty-second notes. In addition, this example incorporates string bends, hammers, pull-offs, and tapping—well, one tap, anyway! You'll find that most of these techniques were employed in previous examples.

This bass part is an excerpt from the bridge of the title tune on my *Pondering the Sushi* CD, immediately following the spacy, harmonically outside section.

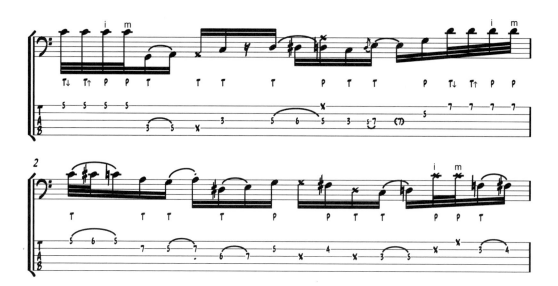

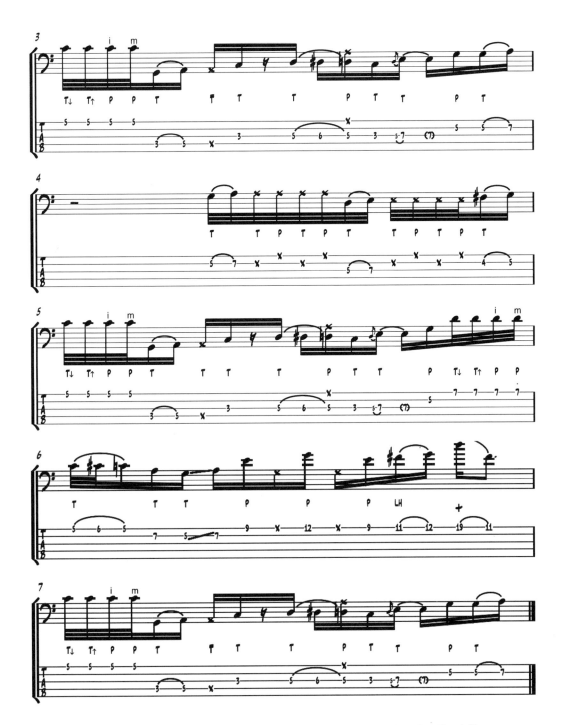

Figure 8-26. Slap Exercise 26 (bridge from "Pondering the Sushi").

You'll see that the part is essentially a four-bar motif with variations. The first and third bars of the phrase are quite similar, while the second and fourth bars incorporate deviations from the motif to varying degrees.

Let's dig into some specifics:

Bar 1 kicks off with the double-thumb/double-pop lick I covered last time. Note the recurrence of that lick on the last eighth note—that is, four thirty-second notes—of the bar. It can lend interest to a part to employ beat displacement: starting recurring parts or motifs in different parts of the measure. Had the lick instead been played starting on the downbeat of bar 2, identical rhythmic placement to bar 1, it would probably have sounded a bit square and overly predictable—at least to my ear.

Additionally, notice the ghosted pop on the G string on the sixteenth note right after beat 3 in bar 1; it rhythmically keeps momentum going over that sustaining slap-note bend. It recurs in the third, fifth, and seventh measures.

Bar 3 is a variation on bar 1: it's identical except for the last eighth note.

Bar 4 incorporates fairly conventional slapping—but in a highly caffeinated state! If you start it slowly and work it up to speed, you'll find that it's not as difficult as it might initially seem.

Bar 5 begins the four-bar phrase again, so is identical to bar 1.

Bar 6 is a variation to the motif; compare it to bar 2. It employs both a string bend—from F♯ to G on the last two sixteenth notes of beat 3—and a right-hand tap/pull-off on beat 4.

Bar 7 is identical to bar 3 and sets up a return to the top of the song.

There you have it! Not too bad, right? I hope this exploration of the slap technique has served to demystify things for those of you who've been apprehensive about slapping. As you can see, it's definitely not, as a drummer friend of mine says, "rocket surgery"!

There are innumerable possible variations to what I've covered, and it's so musically rewarding to come up with lines that are uniquely yours, so use these examples to jump-start your own bass grooves.

And of course, work with a metronome. Particularly relative to slapping, time is everything. Groove profusely!

Let's Grab Coffee: Simplicity

The relatively high notes-per-measure ratio of late sets a good stage for this look into the whole idea of busyness versus sparseness. The appropriate degree of density in our bass lines is dictated by a myriad of factors. These include the musical style of the tune, the orchestration and instrumentation (e.g., what instruments comprise the ensemble and what parts they are playing), the subjective matter of musical taste, and so on.

It cannot be overemphasized that the parts we play should be musically in context with the particular song—unless your intent is to do something quirky or weird, obviously. It's always painful to encounter the inexperienced bassist forcing funk licks into a country tune, or the guy who absolutely can't resist the temptation to demonstrate his command of thirty-second-note altered scale patterns during a contemplative ballad!

As a quick aside, I do want to also reiterate my earlier encouragement regarding those of you whose only musical outlet is the worship set on Sunday mornings to seek other contexts in which to play as well. Not only will you find it invigorating, but the infusion of outside input will also likely enhance what you bring to the worship context. Almost without exception, players I encounter who overplay or are otherwise unintentionally distracting during the worship set are the players who have no other playing opportunity outside of church. They're trying to say *all* they have to say, musically speaking, during those three to five tunes. Everyone loses in that scenario, right?

This chart is for "Mary's Song" from Gina Stockton's *All That I Can Bring* CD—yes, my beautiful wife is also a really talented vocalist and songwriter! This tune is a vocal and piano ballad, and the lyrical subject matter is emotionally heavy, written about Gina's mom's passing.

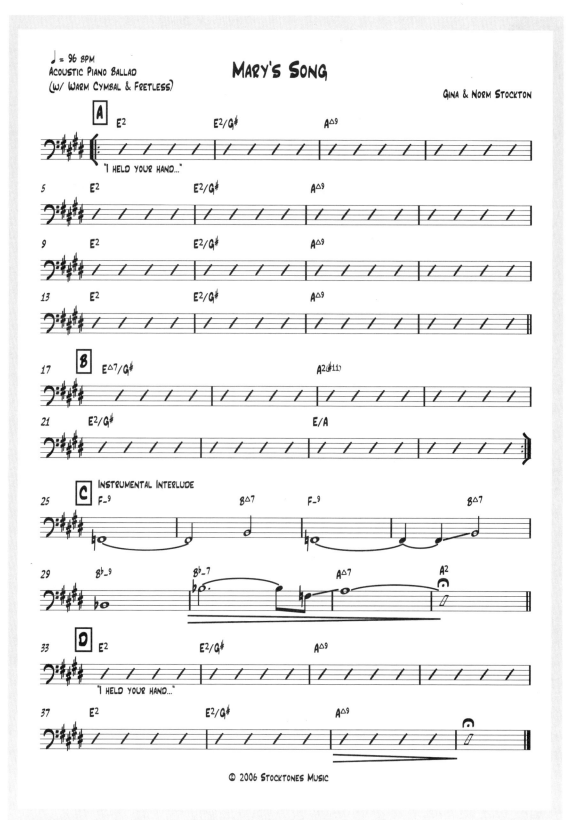

Figure 8-27. "Mary's Song."

With the exception of the transcribed bass line for the bridge at rehearsal mark C, the remainder of the tune—yes, 56 out of 64 measures in the song—involves nothing from the bass. Tacet. At bar 25, the bass line emerges to subtly build the dynamic level under the piano for the brief passage before fading away again at bar 33.

The arrangement and overall emotional statement would have been trampled had I opted to incorporate a bunch of licks—and frankly would have been impaired had I even tried to imply some sort of groove during the section. The most appropriate thing to do in the tune, bass-wise, was to play whole notes and half notes on a fretless bass, tucked in the mix behind the acoustic grand piano. The challenge before me was to place them and phrase them in *just* the right way to enhance the song without distracting.

Let us be encouraged this day to always seek to bring our best musical discernment and taste to our various playing situations, and make it a goal to only play as little—or as much—as necessary to most effectively serve the tune.

9

Bass and Drum Synergy

A groove-oriented approach is one of the most sought-after things that we can bring to a band. To take that to a deeper level: developing vocabulary and synergy with your drummer—allowing the two of you to truly function as a unit—is the ultimate goal. When the bassist and drummer have a deep musical familiarity with each other, are utilizing good listening skills, and are generally interacting effectively, broad smiles are usually the result—liberally distributed throughout the rest of the band, as well as the audience or congregation!

I'd like to share some exercises that target the listening and *spontaneous musical adaptation* skills so essential to achieving this. It's also invaluable for your overall musicality and effectiveness as a bass player to be able to adapt to the changes that are invariably thrown your way on the gig.

Part 1: Let's Talk

The following exercise is to be played with your drummer to help develop a drum-and-bass dialogue—or musical conversation—between the two of you. Before starting, set any volume levels and position yourselves so that you are able to hear each other well.

Here's how it goes:

1. Start by having your drummer call out a random tempo—say, 94 bpm—then dial that up on your hand-held metronome. If you don't already own one, please put down this book and go buy one immediately—if not sooner!

2. Have your drummer start clicking along with the metronome.

3. Now play a spontaneous bass groove. It can be as simple or as involved as you want; just ensure that it's a part, a repeating figure. It can be a one-bar, two-bar, or four-bar phrase—your call—but don't make it any longer than four bars for the purposes of this exercise.

    Note: Feel free to be creative and abandon any preconceived ideas about what the metronome click is implying; it can be clicking on quarter notes, eighth notes, sixteenth notes, triplets, just on the backbeats, or whatever else you decide.

4. Once you've established your part, your drummer will listen, then join in with a corresponding drum groove.

    Note to drummers: It's critical to listen long enough to fully assimilate what's happening with the beat placement, phrasing, and so on—as well as listening for the repeating figure or phrase. If you only listen to the first measure and then join right in, you might not be prepared for whatever variations are introduced later should the bass line involve a longer phrase. If you're having difficulty hearing a repeating figure or the bass line keeps changing, simply listen through another pass until you're clear and/or the bass player solidifies the motif!

5. Once you're both playing your parts, listen to make sure that you're making a solid rhythmic statement together. Make any subtle adaptations of your parts as necessary to enhance the collective statement. Settle in and groove along with each other for a minute or so, keeping your parts more or less intact, with only minor variations thrown in here and there as spice.

6. Now reverse roles and repeat the exercise; this time the drummer establishes the groove, the bassist joins in, and so on. Go back and forth three or four times.

Pretty fun, right?

By the way, it's important to mentally conceive of the part you're going to play before actually putting drumstick to drum head or finger to string. Sing it in your head before executing it on your instrument. In addition to helping you come up with parts that are generally more creative—as they won't be subject to any possible technique limitations—it will also help ensure that once you come in, the first few measures will also sound like music.

Part 2: Curves Ahead

Ready to forge ahead, O Ministers of Groove? How cool is it that we get to practice a craft that is also such a blast to pursue! God is good.

This exercise builds upon the last one. So once you're both comfortable, cohesive, and playing a groove together:

1. You—as the bassist—begin to *morph* your bass part. Specifically, every 8 to 16 bars, incorporate a new variation to your bass line. Make it overt enough that your drummer will definitely recognize that there's a variation happening, but subtle enough that it doesn't completely abandon the original groove; it should still remain recognizable.

     Get creative with the variations, by the way; imagine that the producer or musical director is saying, "That's cool, but could you play it [fill in the blank]?" A partial list to get you started might include:

- mellower/more pensive
- with the same feel but fewer notes/more sparse
- with more of a "pulse" feel/with staccato eighth notes
- driving rock
- sequenced/techno
- more urgent (or more relaxed)
- more riff-oriented
- more harmonically tense (or more "inside")
- funkier, rockier, bluesier, jazzier…and so on.

2. With each new variation, your drummer should alter his or her part to match the new bass statement. For instance, if your variation was to go from bashy rock phrasing to a tight, staccato feel, your drummer might tighten up the hi-hat to go from the big, washy vibe to something more staccato. Depending upon the variation, drum-groove adjustments might include appropriately altering the kick pattern, building or dropping dynamically, hitting an accent on the snare, and so on.

     So essentially, every 16 bars or so, the bass part changes a bit, followed immediately by a corresponding adaptation in the drummer's part.

3. After you've done this for a while, start over again, but reverse the roles. This will allow the two of you to take turns leading with the variations.

Keep in mind that each variation should be introduced one at a time. Additionally, think of it as a loop as opposed to a "moving target" variation: once it's incorporated, keep repeating it with that variation intact so that your rhythm section partner has something he or she can identify and latch onto. This is also good practice for groove retention and sticking to a part.

This type of exercise really helps develop your ear and ability to be a musically responsive and effective bassist. As you and your drummer gain greater familiarity with each other's musical vocabularies, your tightness as a rhythm section will be greatly enhanced.

Part 3: A Focus on Dynamics

One of the most common challenges many musicians experience is maintaining a steady tempo independent of dynamics. More often than not, particularly for less experienced players, the tempo races like mad when the tune starts getting big, then screeches back down to a crawl when the quieter section comes around again. Anyone out there familiar with this phenomenon? I see that hand!

This exercise involves having the drums and the bass play a groove at a reasonably "in your face" dynamic level: good, loud, and punchy.

Keep looping that phrase, while gradually—over the course of four bars or so—bringing it down to a whisper (just *barely* audible) before gradually bringing it back up to bashing. Your neighbors will probably prefer that you do this sometime other than two a.m., by the way! Anyway, practice gradually transitioning back and forth between both extremes of the dynamic range.

The critical part of this exercise is doing all of the above without having *any* effect on the tempo. Set your metronome or click track, and focus on absolute rhythmic consistency.

This transcribed bass line (Figure 9-1) is a fun slap groove that I played while demonstrating this exercise with drummer David Owens in volume 3 of my *Grooving for Heaven* DVD series. Feel free to use it for this exercise—or better yet, come up with something of your own!

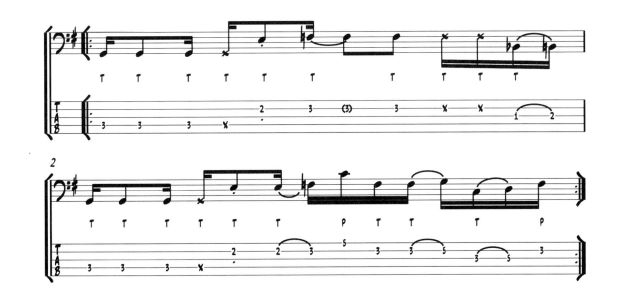

Figure 9-1. Focus: dynamic variation.

Part 4: A Focus on Technique

You and your drummer have hopefully been experiencing progress in your musical interaction as a result of working on these exercises. If not, by the way, don't despair: real musical growth takes time. Keep woodshedding, and you'll most assuredly make headway!

This exercise involves something similar to last time, but instead of using *dynamic* variation, you'll be going back and forth between different *techniques.*

Bassists may experiment with alternating between playing fingerstyle, or slapping, or maybe reggae-style muted thumbing—while drummers might want to go back and forth between grooving on the hat versus the ride, or maybe something primarily involving the toms, or "stirring the soup" on the snare with brushes.

As before, you want to navigate these variations in technique without affecting the tempo. It's really common for the time to either surge or drag when going back and forth between different techniques. Strive to maintain absolute rhythmic consistency regardless of the technique you're employing at any given point.

Figure 9-2. Focus: technique variation.

The line in Figure 9-2 is a simple *ostinato*—or repeating musical phrase—again excerpted from volume 3 of the *Grooving* DVDs with drummer David Owens. In that program, I alternated between fingerstyle and slap while playing this figure. Don't feel constrained to play this specific line, though; create your own part, as long as it allows you to incorporate variations in technique.

This is great stuff for your musicianship. Have fun with those metronomes!

Part 5: Putting It All Together

In this final part, I'd like to suggest a number of variations to take these exercises to the next level.

1. Combine the two previous exercises (from parts 3 and 4), and focus
    on timekeeping regardless of variations in dynamics *and* technique.
    For example, play through Figure 9-3 while alternating back and forth
    every two measures between slapping at a fairly quiet dynamic level and
    fingerstyle at a relatively high dynamic level—while drummers can perhaps
    play a groove based around the ride cymbal at a low dynamic level before
    going to a loud and bashy hi-hat groove.

Figure 9-3. Focus: dynamic and technique variation.

2. As an added element for variation, introduce contrasting *note duration* to the above exercise. For example, play it legato the first time through; then shorten the note duration for a staccato second pass—remembering to keep alternating every other time.

3. As a bassist, it's helpful to practice keeping consistent time regardless of the *note register*. Play through the funky shuffle groove in Figure 9-4 at 90 bpm while incorporating all of the variables in the preceding exercise.

Figure 9-4. Focus: dynamic, technique, note duration, and register variation.

4. For maximum illumination of timekeeping inconsistencies, experiment with slowing the tempo to approximately 60 bpm and simply playing staccato quarter notes, while negotiating variations in dynamics, technique, note duration, and note register from the earlier exercises.

Are you beginning to see the countless potential variations and permutations of these exercises? Try to resist the temptation to work solely on the ones you find easy. Instead, focus on those which you find most challenging to execute well; this approach will maximize the benefits of your time in the woodshed, whether working on these exercises or otherwise.

Along these lines, don't forget to record yourself and listen back with a critical ear. Merciless scrutiny will ensure that you detect your inconsistencies before your colleagues bring them to your attention—which is always preferable!

I hope you and your drummer have found this series helpful for developing and refining your timekeeping effectiveness. Once the two of you are able to negotiate these exercises while maintaining rock-solid time and feel, you'll be well on your way to becoming the foundation of a monster rhythm section!

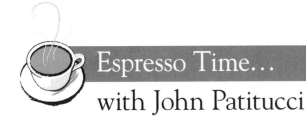

Espresso Time...
with John Patitucci

Quintessential musician whose credits read like a *Who's Who* of modern music. Consummate bassist whose approach has impacted a generation of jazz bass players around the world. Acclaimed sideman as well as successful solo artist. Multiple Grammy-winning player and composer. Highly-respected educator. One could go on and on when attempting to adequately describe John Patitucci's accomplishments in the music world to date. His combination of jaw-dropping technical virtuosity and sheer musicality has truly made him one of the most influential musicians of our time.

Way back in 2002—long before the profound honor of John and his world-class cellist wife, Sachi, contributing their artistry to my *Tea in the Typhoon* CD—I jumped at this opportunity to interview John for *Christian Musician* magazine. It was fantastic to discover that he was also an exceptionally friendly, easygoing, genuinely humble man with a deep love for the Lord. John's insightful perspectives and articulate manner made this interview a real treat—particularly because he had been a hero of mine for years.

Patitucci and his family currently reside in New York. In addition to serving as Associate Professor of Jazz Studies at City College of New York, he tours with the Wayne Shorter Quartet, as well as his own group. Both John and Sachi are also actively involved in the worship ministry at their home church, located north of New York City.

What are your earliest musical recollections?

In the house, my father sang with Mario Lanza records, and he used to like opera a lot—and still does, actually! And I also remember riding around in the car and hearing old Motown records. I have a pretty vivid memory growing up with the music of the '60s and '70s. The first stuff that really impacted me was all of that music coming out of Motown, as well as the Beatles. Then right around the time I started playing bass, I began listening to jazz. I had a box of records from my grandfather that had a bunch of stuff from Wes Montgomery (with Ron Carter and Herbie Hancock), Jimmy Smith Organ Trio records, Ray Charles—it was very inspiring being around so much great music. I remember as an altar boy growing up in the Catholic Church, I was exposed to a lot of the old hymns, too.

Was there any particular music—or maybe even a specific tune—that actually inspired you to pick up the bass in the first place?

I would have to say James Jamerson's playing on "I Was Made to Love Her."

I know that you have formal music education, but there was also a period of time where you were self-taught.

Yeah, when I started out, it was exclusively by ear. My older brother, Tom, played guitar and was initially teaching me how to read and play guitar—but because I'm left-handed, it always felt really unnatural to me for some reason. It was frustrating, because he'd be showing me "Little Brown Jug" out of a Mel Bay book, and here I was not being able to cut it! You know, I'd be trying to count the lines and the spaces. "Wwwwell, I'm not into this." [*Laughs.*] But Tom saw it and very smartly suggested that I try an electric bass instead. It was great: I could use my fingers, it felt natural—and I didn't have to use a pick. So I went on playing by ear. Gradually, he started showing me whatever he was learning on the guitar, and I would adapt it to bass. I did that for a couple years.

Eventually, I met a guy by the name of Chris Poehler who ended up becoming sort of a mentor to me. He's the one who conned me into learning how to read! I'd been playing exclusively by ear and had actually developed a pretty good ear—I could hear things pretty well and had learned a lot of harmony. But Chris got me interested in studying and going to college. I'd already been considering fooling around with the acoustic bass, and by the time I turned 15, I had finally grown tall enough to be able to do it! I eventually studied classical bass at San Francisco State University and Long Beach State University.

I went on to do a ton of recording work in LA, doing a lot of stuff that nobody has ever heard! A lot of R&B-ish, Gospel stuff—very pop. And I enjoyed it a lot; that stuff is part of my roots, even though a lot of people aren't familiar with that part of what I do.

What are some of those projects, for those folks who might want to go track some of them down?

I did sessions for Roby Duke, Bob Bennett, Twila Paris, Chuck Girard…and a bunch of others that, sorry to say, I'm not recalling at the moment. I was doing quite a bit of session work in those days. I was pretty busy, because Abe [Laboriel] could only be in one place at a time. Thankfully, I was picking up some of the work he couldn't do! He was very gracious to help me out. I'm sure he made recommendations on my behalf.

Abe's an incredible guy.

He was a really big encouragement.

You've said that the groove stuff is actually some of your favorite stuff to play.

Yeah, I love that. When I get a call to do that these days, I have a ball.

That seems to be one of the paradoxes: you're a ferocious soloist as well as an incredible groover—yet, because of your reputation as a soloist, you probably miss some calls for groove stuff, don't you?

I think so. There are some false perceptions about music: people think that if someone is able to stretch out a bit and do other things on their instrument, then they *couldn't possibly* have a nice feel, too—because they *know* too much. [*Laughs.*] It's rather ridiculous.

What are your thoughts on the role of the musician in the worship environment?

I think we have a goal to lift people to a higher purpose—to get people into an attitude of praise and worship.

You know, *really*...we should be trying to do that *any* time. Regardless of the geographic location of where we're playing, we still want to bring who we are, and what we believe, and everything about us, to that place where we're playing.

So it doesn't have to be such a delineation. But it does call for a lot more responsibility, because it's easy—and a lot of people make this mistake—to make it where your only outlet for playing music is with your band in church, and you begin to look at it as a gig. It's not just a gig; it's music for the Lord.

When you're playing in a worship setting, from a technical standpoint, do you approach anything differently than when you're in a secular or mainstream environment?

Well, I just play to the tune, whatever the song calls for—whether it's a sparse thing, or whether it needs to be driven a bit more, or if there's singing—I just try to serve that. It just depends upon what's happening, and trying to be sensitive. I really try to make sure that my part isn't distracting, too.

That seems to be the primary musical objective of any worship musician: having the ability to serve the tune and worship time in an effective way, while not being a distraction. To that end, what are your thoughts on the relevance of technical practice for church bassists?

I think the more command, ease, and flexibility you have on your instrument, the better you're able to serve the worship time—because then you won't have to focus all of your attention on, "Okay, I've got to move my finger to the seventh fret now." No, you shouldn't have to even think about that. The goal is to be able to play your instrument without having to focus on the mundane, technical aspects.

This can be a problem sometimes, especially if you're playing a particularly challenging piece. Last weekend at my church, we were playing through some fairly complex, serious stuff and it was a definite challenge, because I was trying to play the piece without getting completely swallowed up by it—you know what I mean? And that can happen with even very simple worship music if the player hasn't been playing the instrument that long and doesn't know the fretboard that well. It's very easy to get distracted with the technical aspects.

So that's the thing—you've got to get comfortable. That doesn't mean that you have to be a virtuoso, but it does mean that you've got to work at it and maybe tell yourself, "Okay, here are the tunes we're playing through this weekend; let me work through them beforehand and make sure I know them really well." I think it's good to spend time and learn the music. If you get different music all the time, just try to be diligent, practice your instrument, and get free on it. Concentrate on trying to worship instead of getting hung up on the mechanics of the bass.

That will help enable you, as a worship leader or facilitator, to somehow make it possible for people to forget about everything else in their lives and concentrate on worshiping—and that's difficult when you're thinking, "Third finger...second finger..." [*Laughs.*] That stuff has got to be out of the way. Let's face it: a lot of the contemporary worship tunes are pretty straightforward—not like "Giant Steps." They're within the capabilities of most players. But it depends upon your attitude. Some people have a bit of a cavalier attitude, where they're just going to "play some music in church." Well, it's a bit more than that, you know? It's a whole lot more than that.

We *all* have to watch out for that. If you do the same thing every week with the same cats—hanging out and having a good time—it's easy for it to become like a gig.

Let's talk about time and groove.

Now we get into the area where it is part knowable and part mystical. [*Laughs.*]

You can't really teach somebody how to groove, but you can certainly point them to all of the records where groove is happening—then they can saturate themselves in that music until it becomes part of them. You can't really impart such an emotional thing. But if they listen enough and play enough, they'll get it. It's impossible to achieve it without listening to the records and getting immersed in the emotional aspect of whatever style you're talking about.

With regard to *time*: you can do more things to work on time. But there's a bunch of different levels of it.

One is that you've got to have *internal* time—so you've got to put in time with a metronome.

But playing with records is good, too, because there's humanity in the sometimes-shifting aspects of time. Time is an agreed-upon thing within the group—it's not just absolute—and in a lot of great music, there has to be room to move within that. Like in classical music, there are a lot of tempos sliding, and waiting for somebody to finish a phrase, then snapping back into tempo. In jazz, there are certainly elements of this, where you're sometimes pushing and playing with a little edge or laying back. But the deal is that you should have control over it. It shouldn't be the instrument pushing you, with you having no causation about it—you just *have* to rush, or *have* to drag. Based on your emotions and what's right for the music, it'll dictate where to put it—and then you've got to have the muscle control to actually do it.

Another point is to develop your internal time so that you don't have to lean on the other musician. For instance, bassists sometimes are too dependent on drummers, to the extent that the drummer feels like they can't ever try other things because the bass line will just fall apart. There should be a sharing of the time, instead of a musician feeling like, "Boy, I'm dragging a truck through cement." [*Laughs.*] With a lot of players, unfortunately, that's their tacit understanding about timekeeping—that it's the drummer's domain. But that's not entirely the case: the feel of the piece is not the same if only the drummer is laying it down and everyone else is sort of bouncing off the surface.

So you have to practice playing with other musicians, and you have to practice playing with a metronome—being good with the click. All of this is especially important if your intent is to make a living as a bassist.

Did you develop your time and feel by woodshedding along with Jamerson records and that sort of thing?

I think the early part of that came from listening to Jamerson, or Ron Carter on all of those old jazz records. It wasn't even about analyzing them empirically, but listening to them about eight million times, you know what I mean? Where it becomes part of you. And where it gets beyond theoretical knowledge to…what it *feels* like. That's super important.

Then the other part of it—the less mystical side of it—is that you have to have enough control over your instrument to make that thing happen. Kinda like Jamerson: he had a great flexibility on the instrument—he could get around. He didn't have any barriers. If he felt like putting something somewhere—feel-wise or otherwise—it was effortless. That's a key thing.

People get confused a lot these days about *technique*. To me, technique isn't real unless it can be put in time and feels good. If you can wiggle your fingers fast, and have "NAMM Show chops," that's not technique. [*Laughs.*] It's just a bad case of the "hoodlies."

Do you have any advice for bassists who find themselves playing with less-experienced drummers where tempos might be shaky? What might a bass player do to help keep a drummer solid or otherwise salvage the ensemble when things are falling apart?

That's a tricky thing. Ultimately, drummers are more powerful, sonically—unless you're playing an electric bass, in which case you could turn up the volume—but that doesn't necessarily solve things if somebody's not sensitive and listening as you try to gently lay it down. Again, it has to be agreed upon and shared. If you're playing with someone who doesn't have a lot of experience and you try to muscle it—and say, "I've *got* it"—it's not going to work without some agreement. If you're playing with a drummer who is dragging, and they're just going down the tubes, your tendency as a young player is usually to try to pull them along. It's very difficult—nearly impossible—unless, again, the drummer is sensitive and willing to go. You can't just pull them into time. It doesn't work that way. I know, because I've tried to do it! [*Laughs.*]

But you *can* gently…kind of, *sit* on things if a drummer is really surging ahead. There's not a whole lot of room to work with before you've got a chasm between the drums and the bass—at that point, it's not about being right or wrong.

You should probably try to make the best of it while you're playing, then find a tactful way to discuss it. I try to phrase things more like, "I think maybe we could put a little more edge into that B-section," or, "Maybe we're letting it drag a bit here, and I'm going to do my best to try to keep the momentum going"—making a point of saying *we* instead of *you*. That seems to work a lot better than saying, "You know what? You're *dragging* there!"

"Maybe if *we* hit our hi-hat in *this* manner...."
[*Laughs.*] Yeah, it's always helpful to try to make it a "team thing."

It's something that should be talked about, but it shouldn't be *over*talked about, if you know what I mean. If you talk about it *too* much, then people get freaked out and they try to think too much—and it never feels right after that!

Your instructional videos, *Electric Bass, Volumes 1 and 2*, are fantastic. Are there any other resources you've found helpful—particularly in the area of improvisation?
Thanks. I'd say study Bach's music. In terms of learning how to compose better bass lines—whether they're walking bass lines or otherwise—listen to baroque music, or Bach's *Brandenburg Concertos*, Vivaldi's music—anything where there's a continuo— and see how they outline the chords.

For ear training, David Baker's put out some great stuff. *The Jazz Theory Book* by Mark Levine is nice—very organized and useful for expanding your harmonic understanding. *Any* of the books by Chuck Sher are high quality and well thought-out—very good stuff.

In terms of broad groove playing, I don't know that there's a lot of material out there, book-wise. It's really about *Go-get-a-James-Brown-collection-and-learn-every-groove-off-of-it*! There is that James Jamerson thing, *Standing in the Shadows of Motown*, where every hit he ever played on is written out. If you don't know how to read music, then go get the records! There are a lot of different things you can study. Check out Willie Weeks on *Donnie Hathaway Live*. . . . I could go down the list.

In terms of your Brazilian and African influences, were there any resources you went to, or was it more of that *immersion* thing that you were describing earlier?
Yeah, it was that immersion thing, plus I learned a lot of stuff from players I know—like Armand Sabal-Lecco. There's one record that I'd definitely recommend for anyone

interested in getting into African music: Salif Keita's *Soro*. It's incredible—that one inspired me a lot. There's a book by Oscar Stagnaro about Brazilian and African music which is great—*The Latin Bass Book: A Practical Guide*. I highly recommend it. Also, Cliff Korman and Nelson Faria have a new book out, called *Inside the Brazilian Rhythm Section*, which is *very* cool.

How many hours a day are you playing these days?

It varies. It really depends upon where I am: When I'm on tour, I'll play a couple hours for the show, plus soundchecks and rehearsals. When I'm at home, sometimes I don't get a chance to practice until late at night, once the kids are in bed. It really varies.

Do you try to practice every day?

At this point, it's not always a reality. I'd *like* to. Sometimes it's more like, "Okay—they're in bed" and I'll practice for three hours. Other times, I'll go for days without practicing—but I'm gigging, etc.

When I was younger, it was constant—hours and hours. And I think that's essential; you have to put that time in. As a young person learning their instrument, there's no negotiating that part.

At the peak of your early days of woodshedding, how much time were you putting in a day?

Probably around six hours a day. Lots of gigging with different groups, as well as practicing.

Have you ever experienced any playing-related hand or arm problems?

I've been pretty fortunate. I think there was one time, when I was with Chick [*Corea*] and we were just going crazy—playing all the time with the Akoustic band. I somehow strained something in my right hand and had to chill out for a little while. But haven't really had any problems since then.

Do you have any sort of warm-up or stretching regimen that you go through?

Not really.

So you're just genetically *happening*.

[*Laughs.*] Sometimes I do the thing where you hold your hand with your fingers aiming up—like you're saying "hi" to someone—and you take your other hand and bend the tops of those fingers back and stretch them.

Now that I'm a little older, I'm noticing that stuff doesn't naturally stay as loose. It's been 32 years [*c. 2002*] since I first picked up the electric bass, so I've been playing for a long time. I have to watch things and take care of myself a bit more now.

Congratulations on your Grammy nomination [Best Instrumental Composition] for the title track from your *Communion* CD. What an astounding piece of music.

Thank you very much; it was nice to be nominated. Those were almost exclusively people from our church who played on it, other than Branford [*Marsalis, soprano sax*] and Brad [*Mehldau, piano*].

It was incredibly emotional—a very moving composition and performance. It was also really interesting how it transitioned from the string-quartet vibe to more of a jazz ballad, with upright and soprano sax.

Thanks; it was a lot of fun to do. I'm actually working on a record right now called *Songs, Stories & Spirituals* that will also include string quartet and other stuff along those lines. It will feature Brian Blade; John Thomas; Tom Patitucci; my wife, Sachi Patitucci; Ed Simon; Luciana Souza; and a number of other fantastic musicians who also played on the last album. Brazilian stuff, lots of singing…should be good. I'm going to keep trying to expand my orchestrational side as far as some of the things you were describing from *Communion*.

Looking forward to it! By the way, what an absolute luxury to have players of that caliber on your worship team.

Yeah, it's pretty wild!

I've got to also mention one of your earlier projects, *Heart of the Bass*. That has to be one of my favorite projects ever. The writing and performances were so passionate and emotive.

Thank you…yeah, that project was actually done during a *really* difficult time in my life. I was going through a definite "valley experience"—and I'm not talking about the San Fernando Valley! [*Laughs.*] In addition, I didn't do a lot of the writing on that project—most of the pieces were written by others—and schedules worked out such that I was rushing to learn a lot of that music at the last minute. So it was a rough time.

But as far as the performances, I always just try to be transparent and get out of the way, so to speak.

How did you come to faith?

I grew up as a Catholic, but eventually started asking a lot of questions for which the priests didn't seem to have good answers. I was really searching. When I was a teenager—by this time, we'd moved out to California—I was drafted by my teachers to play in this big band that they had at night. There were several members who were Christians, including the pianist, who was the music minister at his church. He befriended me and used to hire me to come and play at his church. There was a bunch of young people there who were actually *happy* at church! There seemed to be a real joy. I remember talking to my friend over a period of time and asking a lot of questions. I wanted to be close to God, but I'd never really known anything about having a relationship with God, or how to study the Bible, etc. And that summer, I got saved.

That's awesome, John. Thanks so much for taking time out of your busy schedule to share your thoughts and heart with us. Do you have anything else you'd like to add in closing?

Thank you. If I could offer any parting words of advice, I'd say: keep diligent in your faith as a Christian to ensure that your spiritual identity never gets swallowed up by your identity as a musician. God bless you. . . .

Visit John at www.johnpatitucci.com.

A SELECTED DISCOGRAPHY

All as leader:

- *Remembrance*
- *Line by Line*
- *Songs, Stories & Spirituals*
- *Communion*
- *One More Angel*
- *Heart of the Bass*

10

The Tap Technique

If you've read up to this point in the book, you will probably attest to my passion for ensemble bass. I can't overemphasize the importance of having a firm grasp on solid fundamental grooving before delving into the ancillary areas of bassdom. Ignoring this will greatly increase the likelihood of getting relieved of your bass-playing duties at some point—probably in a sudden and unpleasant manner! By the way, my preface from the opening section of "The Slap Technique" chapter applies here as well.

So it's upon the bedrock of supportive ensemble bass playing that this exploration of the tap technique begins. Tapping produces a really interesting timbre and is quite fun to employ once in a while. In the right hands, it can be incredibly musical—Michael Manring and Brian Bromberg both come to mind—but there's also the potential for it to sound sterile, harsh, and/or utterly ostentatious.

Let's work up the basic mechanics of the technique and then spend some time exploring musical applications, variations, and creative options.

Part 1

The fundamental technique is a percussive motion where your fingertip strikes and frets the string without plucking it.

With your left or fretting hand, it's essentially just a matter of fretting the note, but with a bit of a percussive, "hammer" type of attack. It's also important to employ a relatively flat left hand to facilitate muting; the muting burden on your fretting hand is increased due to limited availability of the right hand to assist.

The right-hand technique involves pressing the string down to the fretboard with a percussive striking motion as well—*just* hard enough so that the note will ring. I've found that anchoring my right thumb on the top edge of the fingerboard can help with both dynamic consistency and accuracy.

Speaking of which, you'll definitely want to ensure that both your right and left hands are tapping with about the same amount of force so there aren't major dynamic inconsistencies between the two—for example, thunderous volume with your right-hand taps and barely audible blips from your left hand.

Once you're comfortable with the basic feel of tapping single notes with either hand, give Exercise 1 (Figure 10-1) a try. In addition to helping solidify the mechanics, it will also assist in developing independence between hands.

Figure 10-1. Tap Exercise 1.

Please refer to the note above the written exercise to clarify the musical nomenclature. It actually looks more complicated than it really is. Harmonically, you're just working with roots and fifths. You'll notice that the first bar of the phrase is simply octaves. The second bar repeats the left-hand pattern of the first bar, but rhythmically displaces the right-hand pattern by an eighth note—so the right hand *answers* the left-hand phrase in bar 2.

While I've not specified a particular fingering, the most comfortable fingering assignment for me involves my left-hand index and pinky fingers (at the 5th and 7th frets, respectively) and my right-hand index and ring fingers (at the 12th and 14th frets). This seems to best facilitate both tapping and any necessary muting.

Once you've assimilated Exercise 1, practice it with a drum machine and/or metronome to ensure rhythmic solidity, making sure that the dynamic level between notes is even.

Part 2

This exercise takes the introductory tap pattern from last time to the next level. Keep in mind that the focus is still simply on getting the basic mechanics together; creative musical application is coming soon!

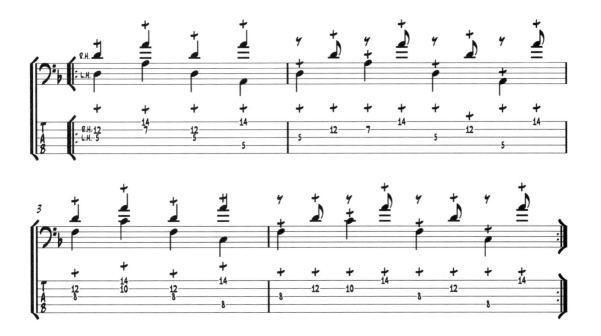

Figure 10-2. Tap Exercise 2.

You'll notice that the first two bars of Exercise 2 are identical to the previous exercise, while the third and fourth bars transpose the left- or fretting-hand pattern up the neck a minor third, or three frets.

There's no alteration to the rhythmic pattern or basic motif, so this should feel pretty comfortable after a couple of run-throughs. This exercise introduces another level of independence between right and left hands, which is essential for getting your tap technique together.

As before, pay special attention to keeping the dynamic level similar between your right and left hands; if you notice certain notes are consistently much louder or quieter than the others, take some time to adjust the amount of force you're using with that finger. There shouldn't be a noticeable difference in volume or tone between right- or left-hand taps.

My suggested fingering for this exercise is the same as last time: left-hand index and pinky fingers and right-hand index and ring fingers.

Once you've got Exercise 2 under your fingers, it's time to turn on that metronome—you knew that was coming, right?—and make sure the time is solid!

Part 3

Continuing on with variations to the recurring motif from last time, the goal remains getting the basic mechanics together, but while also working toward greater independence between the two hands—we're multitasking! This variation will only be rhythmic; you'll be using the same notes as in the previous exercise.

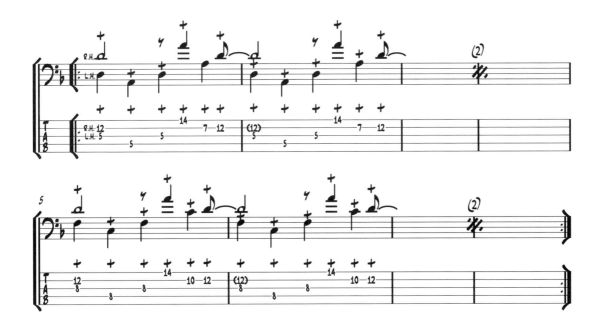

Figure 10-3. Tap Exercise 3.

Don't forget that the *stems-down* notes are played with the left or fretting hand, while the *stems-up* ones are for the right hand. You might find it helpful to isolate each and play through the exercise a couple of times that way before tackling the two together.

Don't worry if it initially gives you that rubbing-stomach-while-patting-head kind of feeling. With a bit of practice, it will definitely get much more comfortable—and actually become fun!

Once you're able to successfully make it through a couple of play-throughs, turn on the metronome and focus on rhythmic solidity.

Part 4

Once again, you're basically using the same notes as last time—but this exercise rhythmically mixes things up a bit, particularly with respect to the right hand.

As with earlier exercises, it can be helpful to initially isolate each hand's part and play through a couple of times before merging the two parts together.

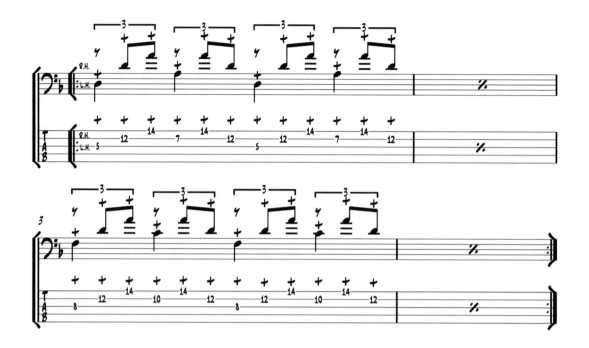

Figure 10-4. Tap Exercise 4.

The left-hand part is simply root–fifth–root–fifth with a modulation of the pattern up a minor third in the second half of the exercise. The right-hand pattern is interspersed between the left-hand part and involves just two notes—alternating from ascending to descending.

After a couple of successful play-throughs, you'll discover that it actually looks more difficult than it really is. Have fun!

Part 5

I hope the basic mechanics of the tap technique are starting to feel natural and comfortable for you. Learning tapping or any other technique requires consistent and focused practice. For those who might be struggling a bit, please don't get discouraged; it will definitely come together with repetition.

This exercise is a natural progression from the last one. While the notes are different, the actual tapping pattern is only a slight variation from before.

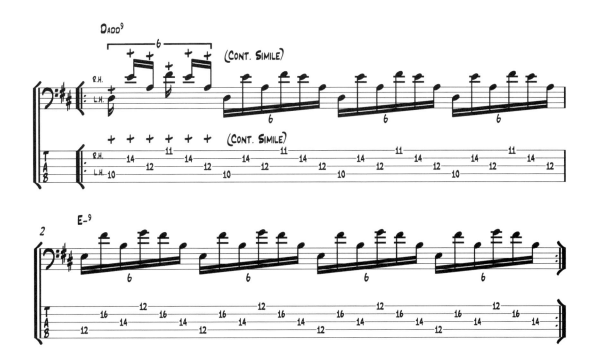

Figure 10-5. Tap Exercise 5.

Once again, the *stems-down* notes are played with the left or fretting hand and the *stems-up* ones are for the right hand. This pattern is only reflected in the first beat of bar 1—for clarity and ease of reading—but should continue through the remainder of the exercise.

You'll be going back and forth between playing D(add9) and Em9. The pattern in the first bar covers the root note (D), fifth, ninth, and third—or tenth, as it's played an octave above the root note. The second bar includes the root note (E), fifth, ninth, and minor third—similarly up an octave.

And yes, the "theory police" are correct—that E-9 is technically an E-(add9), as you're not playing the flatted-seventh. Let's not split hairs!

Rhythmically, it's helpful to think of the pattern as triplets, with the first note of each triplet alternating back and forth between the root (which I usually play with my left index finger) and the third (usually played with my left ring finger). The left- or fretting-hand pattern is quite similar to earlier exercises in this series but involves different strings.

The right-hand pattern is repetitive and always descending—the ninth followed by the fifth. My preference is to play those notes with my right-hand ring and index fingers, respectively.

Once you play through this exercise slowly a few times, you'll likely find it coming together pretty quickly. As before, it will then be time to turn on the metronome and make sure that it's rhythmically and dynamically even and consistent. Tear it up!

Part 6

Here's a different approach to tapping from the exercises so far. I employ it in more of a single-string context—in the vein of what rock-guitar icon Eddie Van Halen unleashed in his "Eruption" masterpiece to send legions of guitar players to the woodshed!

I personally don't do this type of tapping that often, primarily due to the fact that it tends to be the least effective of the various applications for continuing to hold down the bottom end; it definitely takes on more of a lead guitar vibe. However, it is an interesting use of the technique to have available should the music ever dictate. Bass phenom Billy Sheehan has done some absolutely jaw-dropping things with this approach.

I employed it on a line toward the end of my solo version of "The Star Spangled Banner"—the "O'er the land of the free" phrase—and that line is transcribed in the written example. A video clip is posted on YouTube if you'd like to see and hear it; the part occurs at 1:41 running time.

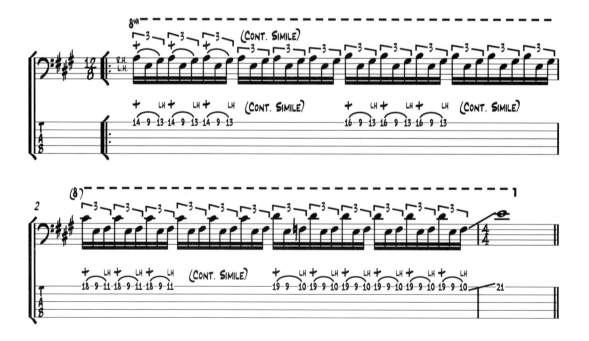

Figure 10-6. Tap Exercise 6.

It involves a combination of tapping, pull-offs, and hammers. All of this activity is focused on the high G string. Here is clarification of the technique nomenclature that appears above the tablature staff in the written example:

- **+:** right-hand tap (I used my index finger in this example) followed immediately by a *pull-off*—instead of vertically releasing the index finger from the tapped note, the string is *pulled* laterally so the release generates a separate plucked note.
- **L.H.:** left-hand tap—or hammer-on—a percussive tapping of a note higher on the string than the one being fretted.

It's actually quite simple: the basic repeating figure is a triplet, with the first note being a right-hand tap, followed by a pull-off to the second note, which is already fretted (in this example, by my left index finger) followed by a left-hand hammer-on (in this example, by either my pinky, ring, or middle finger, depending upon the stretch required to play the figure). Each phrase is played rapidly six times before the notes change.

It's really much easier than the written notation might suggest. Start slowly to get the basic mechanics together before working it up to speed. Ensure that the dynamic level (apparent loudness) from note to note is as even as possible.

By the way, the *8va* simply indicates that the notes are to be played an octave higher than written. This is done to simplify reading by avoiding a truckload of ledger lines!

Part 7

I've covered several different approaches to the tap technique so far. Here's another version I employ that is a bit of a combination of the ones previously covered. It was used extensively on the B-section of a tune from my *Pondering the Sushi* project called "Come Before Winter"; I'll be specifically looking at that in part 8.

This approach involves tapping based upon arpeggio figures, but also incorporates some pull-offs with the right hand. This is perhaps my favorite method of employing the tap technique—particularly when doing unaccompanied solo playing.

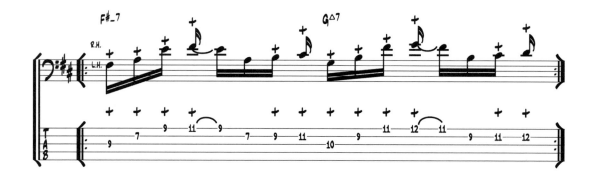

Figure 10-7. Tap Exercise 7.

This exercise involves playing through a vamp between F#-7 and GM7. You'll notice the basic pattern starts with left-hand taps of the first three notes—the root, flatted-third, and flatted-seventh tapped by my middle, index, and ring fingers, respectively. A right-hand tap (I use my index finger) is next, followed by a pull-off and *rake* (a pluck of the note on the next lower string) and concluding with a left-hand tap and right-hand tap. The figure is then transposed up to GM7.

Almost sounds like music, right? Once you play through it a few times, you'll discover—as with many of these exercises—that it also looks more difficult than it really is. Hang in there and have fun!

Part 8

The final tapping example I'd like to share with you comes from the tune "Come Before Winter" from my *Pondering the Sushi* CD. As I mentioned above, this approach combines some of the ideas I've covered so far. It incorporates some pull-offs with the right hand as you melodically and harmonically navigate your way through several arpeggio forms. I really enjoy this approach to tapping when unaccompanied—or very sparsely accompanied—playing is called for.

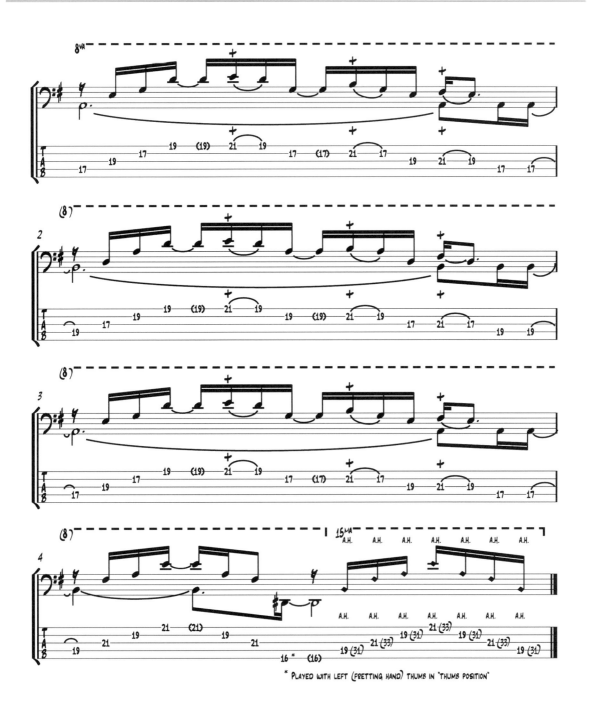

Figure 10-8. Tap Exercise 8.

In the written exercise, you're basically playing through a vamp between A-7 and B-7, although the tap figure adds various upper extensions such as ninths and elevenths. The initial ascending part of the line (the first four notes of each measure) are actually plucked by the right hand in a normal "guitar-esque" fingerpicking manner, while the remainder of the pattern involves right-hand taps (I used my index finger), pull-offs, and rakes, plucking the note on the next-lower string. Once plucked, the notes fretted by the left hand are held for the remainder of the bar—so the rest of the motion in that bar is entirely executed by the right hand.

The only exceptions to the above are two little twists I threw in on the fourth measure:

- The D♯ bass note on the second half of that bar—raising the minor third of B-7 to a major third—was played with my left thumb in *thumb position*, similar to what acoustic bassists use in higher neck positions. This is definitely extra credit; don't beat yourself up if your hands complain a bit over this one!
- The artificial harmonics that occur immediately after that D♯ : I haven't covered those yet, but stay tuned, as they're coming up in the next chapter!

O Purveyors of Fine Groove! I hope this exploration of the tap technique has been both fun and helpful for expanding your palette on the bass. In the worship context, I might only employ this technique once in a great while—to very lightly slur into a single higher note that I can't reach with my fretting hand at the end of a tune, for instance. In that example, I would likely turn my fingerboard away from the congregation toward the drummer to avoid the "hey check this out" vibe.

That said, your musicianship benefits nonetheless from having tapping among your available timbres should the song dictate—whether that means something understated or otherwise. As you prepare to move on, I encourage you to ensure that songcentric, ensemble-oriented approach to your playing remains firmly intact. Please don't become another casualty of bombastic and inappropriate "tappity-clackity-slappities"; the world is unfortunately full of such players who briefly impress but can't get a gig!

11

Chimes, Thuds, and Swells: The Expanded Palette

Welcome back to the woodshed! While I'm on the topic of exploring the incredibly diverse range of sounds within the bass guitar's capabilities, I'd like to share a couple of other techniques to broaden the sonic palette when the music calls for it.

Artificial Harmonics

One of those techniques is *artificial harmonics*, which was deferred from my analysis of the tune "Come Before Winter" in the last chapter.

Most of you are likely already familiar with the sound of harmonics, whether from recordings or tuning up your bass (or guitar; I know a bunch of you defected from that camp!)

To give context, let's first briefly address *natural harmonics*. They can be easily found by lightly resting your fretting-hand finger on any string directly above the fifth, seventh, or twelfth frets, without actually fretting the note, and then plucking the string in the normal manner. This type of harmonic can be found in many other places on the fretboard as well. They have a delicate, chimelike tone that can be really beautiful. Legendary bassist Jaco Pastorius possessed an encyclopedic knowledge of the placement of all the natural harmonics on the fretboard—to the extent that he could play intricate melodies using them exclusively. The challenge for the rest of us mere mortals is that this type of harmonic falls on the fingerboard in a nonintuitive manner: their pattern has almost nothing in common with the layout of fretted notes.

By recreating the physics of natural harmonics but using a *fretted* string—as opposed to an open string—one can generate harmonics of *any* desired note. Harmonics generated this way are referred to as artificial harmonics. They are a lot easier to use instinctively—in the moment—because they fall in a manner consistent with the fretted notes on the fingerboard. Let's dip our toes in the water.

Part 1

As reflected in Figure 11-1, to play a high-octave harmonic C using artificial harmonics, I would fret the C at the 17th fret of the G string, then lightly rest my right- or plucking-hand index finger at the midpoint between that fretted note and the bridge saddle—which would technically be right above the 29th fret if our fingerboards could accommodate it.

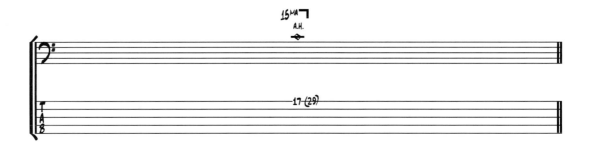

Figure 11-1. Exercise 1: Artificial harmonic.

In my own approach to this technique, I use my right middle finger to pluck the string immediately behind my index finger—or more specifically, behind the point at which my index finger is touching the string.

By the way, that high C is up in Guitarsville and a solid argument could be made to reflect it in treble clef. That said, we're all *bass players*—so for ease of reading, the *15ma* note reflects that a passage is to be played two octaves higher than written—sort of like a double 8va.

Anyway, get comfortable with the basic mechanics by experimenting with fretting any note, and locating the octave harmonic by splitting the distance between the fretted note and the point at which the string touches the bridge. It's a bit easier when the notes are higher on the fretboard. Try fretting the 9th fret of the G string and finding its artificial harmonic at the 21st fret of that same string, and so on.

Isn't it cool having access to notes that are in a much higher register than one would typically associate with a bass guitar?

Part 2

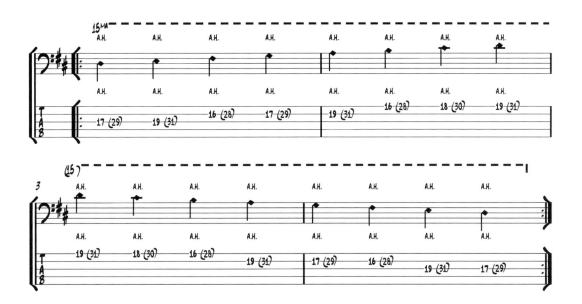

Figure 11-2. Exercise 2: Artificial harmonics.

Let's expand on the technique by applying it to a scale.

The D major scale falls in a good range on the fretboard for this purpose. As reflected in the written exercise, you'll fret it starting on the 17th fret of the A string. The previous exercise in Part 1 revealed that the artificial harmonic for the note one octave above a fretted note can be found at the midpoint between that fretted note and the bridge saddle. In this case, that's again right around the 29th fret—approximating where that would fall if our fingerboards extended that high.

Eyeballing it as best you can, rest your right- or plucking-hand index finger lightly on the A string and pluck—again, I use my right middle finger for this—directly behind that point. If your index finger is correctly placed, you'll hear a clear and bell-like D an octave higher than the D you're fretting with your left hand.

As a quick aside, I encourage you to experiment with your right index-finger placement and incrementally move it from a point too close to the bridge to gradually being too far from the bridge toward the neck. Notice how the note appears when you find the sweet spot, then fades away when you leave it? I think it's really helpful to practice finding the artificial harmonics for random notes on the fretboard in this manner.

Getting back to the scale: once you've found that D harmonic, fret the E at the 19th fret of the A string and pluck the artificial harmonic for that note. Continue up to the D and G strings and repeat the technique for the rest of the D major scale.

You'll find that the closer to the bridge you are with your right hand, the tighter the spacing is between the notes. Even though there may be 1 to 1 1/2 inches between D and E at the 17th and 19th frets on the fretboard, that distance is reduced to about 1/2 inch or so up where your right index finger is locating the artificial harmonic. If you extended it the full 1 1/2 inch or so, it would end up being much closer to the bridge saddle than that halfway point I've been discussing.

If you imagine extending the fingerboard up so it accommodated a full three-octave range of 36 frets, that highest octave would be spaced really tightly compared to the low octave, right? It's the same idea.

Once you get to the high D at the 19th fret of the G string, descend through the scale as reflected in bars 3 and 4.

Play this exercise as slowly as necessary to get the harmonic to voice cleanly and with little, if any, of the actual fretted note sounding. The fretted note would be clearly apparent as an octave lower than the intended harmonic. Once you have it under your fingers, practice it along with a metronome to ensure that rhythmic accuracy and consistency is happening.

Part 3

I hope you've been enjoying this foray into the expanded palette—some of the extra stuff that's nice to be able to apply to musical situations with taste and discernment!

As with any technique, artificial harmonics are best assimilated into our musical bags by being practiced in a broad range of ways—such as scales, arpeggios, melodies, and so on. This tends to make it where we can truly let the music dictate the appropriate technique in the moment.

To this end, I'd like you to work through that D major scale again—but utilizing staggered thirds this time (Figure 11-3). As you may recall from the "Fingerboard Familiarity" chapter, this approach incorporates intervallic jumps that serve a number of purposes, including introducing string skipping and helping us assimilate scales by not always approaching them in a linear manner—all while sounding a bit more like music!

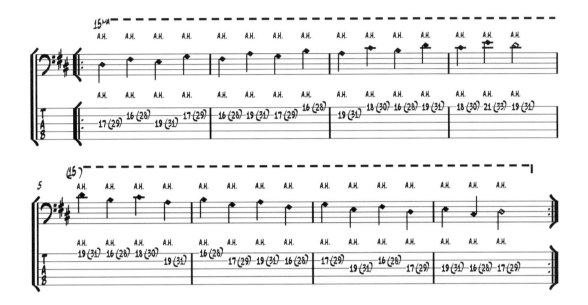

Figure 11-3. Exercise 3: Artificial harmonics.

You'll be playing the scale in the same position as last time but adding the relative third to each degree of the scale. Starting on the first scale degree, D, you'll follow that with the third; then proceed to the second scale degree, E, and follow that with the fourth; and so on.

It ends up being: 1-3, 2-4, 3-5, 4-6, 5-7, 6-8, 7-9, 8 (octave).

Then descending: 8-6, 7-5, 6-4, 5-3, 4-2, 3-1, 2-7 (in the octave below the root), 1.

As before, strive to minimize the sound of the actual fretted note—an octave below the intended artificial harmonic—as you play through this exercise. It takes a bit of experimenting to find the exact placement of the octave harmonic with the right or plucking hand. Take a moment to find it again if you get lost, starting by plucking near the bridge and gradually moving toward the fingerboard until the octave harmonic jumps out. If you go too far, it will disappear again.

Part 4

I trust that the basic mechanics of the artificial-harmonics technique are coming together and feeling comfortable. Now for a bit of *actual* musical application!

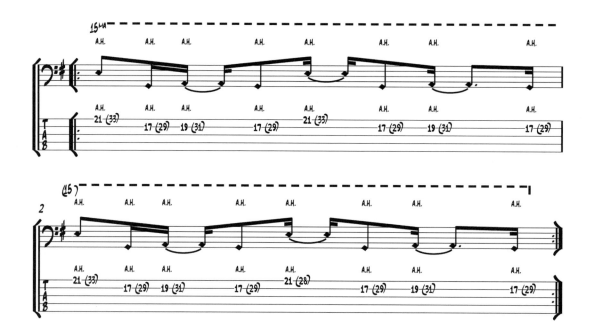

Figure 11-4. Exercise 4 (excerpt from "Come Before Winter").

I used a variation for this excerpt of one of the layered parts on "Come Before Winter" from my *Pondering the Sushi* project (Figure 11-4); it first occurs at 1:05 into the track and is panned slightly to the left.

Almost all of the line employs the technique as covered in early exercises, except the last sixteenth note of beat 2 in the second measure. You'll notice that note is an even higher artificial harmonic than the octaves you've been playing. It's actually a fifth and can be found by plucking the harmonic located two and a half steps lower on the fingerboard than our usual octave harmonic. Specifically, I'm fretting the note at the 21st fret, the octave is directly over the 33rd fret—or where the 33rd fret would hypothetically occur if my fingerboard extended that high—so that harmonic for the fifth would be at the hypothetical 28th fret. It might take a moment to locate the precise position to get that note to sound.

On a parenthetical note, I wish I could say that I'm just a brilliantly creative guy and located that one specific note after methodically searching it out—but in reality, I stumbled upon it while experimenting and thought, "Hey—what was *that?*" That fifth is up in the stratosphere for a bass guitar, and I thought it brought something interesting to that section of the tune.

None of this is nuclear physics; *you* can make cool discoveries just by experimenting around with this too! The overtone series present on your open strings is present on your fretted notes as well, so if you're so inclined, explore freely. Experiment with artificial harmonics, and even combine them with your knowledge of natural harmonics to give yourself a broad assortment of notes that you can play with that harmonic timbre.

Quiet intros and outros or breakdown sections of tunes can be good places to employ them without abandoning your role as the bass player. Just remember that erring on the side of subtlety and understatement will usually serve you and the music well; in other words, don't feel the need to turn every quiet musical moment into a chime-fest!

Muted Thumb

Let's move on to the muted thumb; you might recall I briefly covered it in the Reggae section of the "Musical Styles" chapter. What began almost exclusively as a staple tone of the reggae bassist can now be heard in a broad spectrum of musical genres.

Part 1

Tonally, it's a warm and muted "thud," rather than a bright, ringing, pianolike tone. I love the contrast and find lots of uses for it.

The actual technique is fairly simple and primarily a function of the plucking hand, although the fretting hand can definitely tweak it as well. It involves lightly resting the fleshy part of your palm on the strings right near the bridge saddles while plucking notes with your thumb.

The attack and sustain can be fairly drastically altered by how hard you pluck, whether you pluck with the soft part of your thumb or get a bit of fingernail involved, how much pressure you exert on the strings with your palm, and how close or far from the bridge saddles you rest your palm. The effect can be further intensified by also lightly resting the unused fingers of your fretting hand across the strings. The timbre can range from the classic reggae tone to emulations of an upright bass or an old Hofner Beatle bass. I encourage you to experiment and get a feel for how to achieve different tone variations with your particular instrument.

Once you're feeling comfortable, check out Exercise 5 for a sample of its musical application. The line outlines the chord progression while remaining sparse enough to leave some nice space in an arrangement.

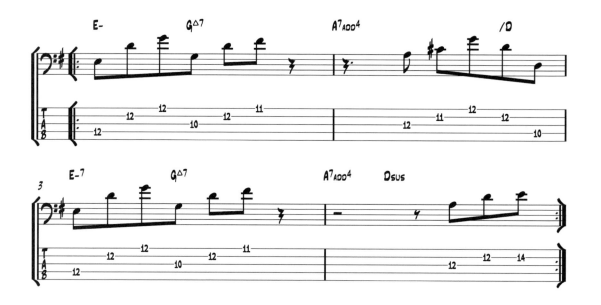

Figure 11-5. Exercise 5: Muted thumb.

Part 2

Exercise 6 is an application of the technique as a steady stream of eighth notes under a chord progression.

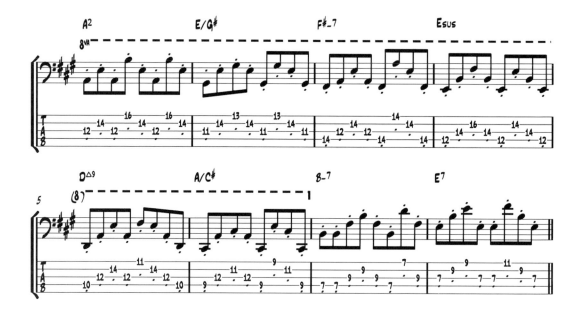

Figure 11-6. Exercise 6: Muted thumb.

The actual fingering pattern varies, as it was transcribed from an improvised example on my *Pondering Bass Technique* DVD. Feel free to pick a pattern from one measure and impose it over the entire exercise or, alternatively, use the written example as a springboard for your own patterns.

Remember to keep the notes very short (staccato) and tweak your technique to achieve that warm and muted thud tone. After getting it under your fingers, play it along with a metronome to ensure rhythmic accuracy and consistency.

By the way, record yourself if possible and listen back to ensure that it both sounds as you're intending and is locking with the click. This is another element of that "eating your veggies" aspect of developing one's musicianship: not as much fun, but enormously helpful for your musical growth!

Combining Techniques

Hopefully this exploration of varied timbres available to us as bassists—without even necessitating a tweak of the tone knob!—is going well and inspiring your own ideas in terms of musical application.

I really enjoy *combining* various techniques in the pursuit of creating musically interesting parts. As my goal is to stretch your musicianship and help illuminate the possibilities, many of the following examples are fairly involved. However, the underlying concept—having a broad palette of "colors" at your disposal should the musical needs dictate—is applicable to everything from a fusion gig to jamming in your bedroom to Sunday morning services. Context remains paramount: constantly assess the arrangement and overall musical vibe of the moment to make sure that your part is serving the music. Don't find yourself being one of those players who always sounds like you're seeking attention. Effective ensemble playing involves knowing when to be overt and when to disappear into the musical tapestry.

Part 1

With that in mind, let's take a look at one way to mix things up a bit. Figure 11-7 is a transcription of the basic A-section groove from "Blessed" from my *Pondering the Sushi* CD.

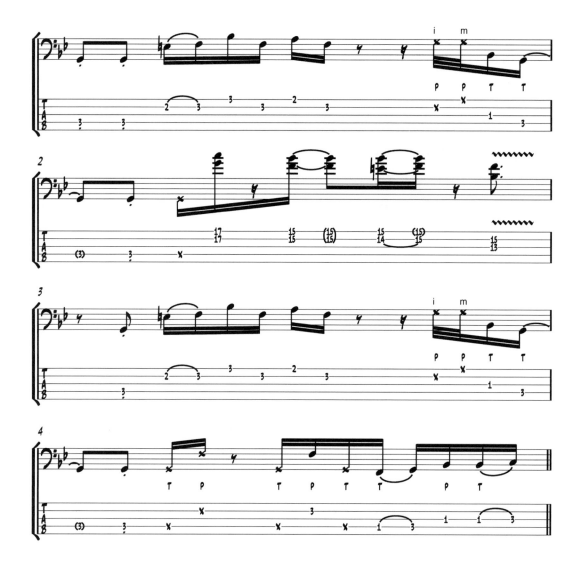

Figure 11-7. Exercise 7 (excerpt from "Blessed").

The sixteenth notes are shuffled in this groove. The song is essentially a bass-and-drum jam—with a piano joining in for the B-section—so there's a lot of sonic space for the bass. This bass line emulates an ensemble playing a groove by jumping registers, switching up timbres through technique variations, and generally approaching things as a tapestry of parts. A more intensive look at the full section, with melody and the various embellishments, is upcoming later in this chapter.

You might find this example challenging to play if you don't have a lot of experience with the various techniques utilized, but don't get discouraged. Work it up slowly, and you'll be surprised by how quickly things come together. If necessary, simplify any passages that you find challenging. The more important point is starting to develop a feel for seamlessly incorporating different elements into the groove.

The low part is played using the muted-thumb technique and is employed on the first three beats of bars 1 and 3. I use my right thumb to play both the low-G eighth notes on the E string and the proceeding E hammering to the F on the D string. Make sure to keep your right palm on the strings back by the bridge to maintain the same muted timbre on the higher strings.

You'll see that the slap technique is applied to the last beat of bars 1 and 3, as well as most of bar 4. The *i* and *m* pops are basically the flam type of effect popularized by the amazing Victor Wooten. It is accomplished by playing a muted pop with both the right index and middle fingers in quick succession. A rolling motion with the right hand helps with this.

The double-stops in bar two simulate what a guitarist might play in this sort of groove. I use my right index and middle fingers to execute those.

The key to playing a part like this well is to ensure that the time is consistent regardless of the technique being employed. It's a particularly common tendency for players to fluctuate the tempo when making the transition between different techniques. Once you have the basic components together, work it up with a metronome—and be merciless!

Part 2

Here's a groove that incorporates slapping, chording, and harmonics (Figure 11-8). This particular example is well suited for playing with just a drummer, as it doesn't leave a lot of room for other instruments! Again, feel free to simplify any especially challenging parts; the important point is to see how different techniques might be combined in musically creative ways.

Figure 11-8. Exercise 8: Combining techniques.

Before I get into the specifics, it might be helpful to get a general overview of the part. You'll notice that it's basically a two-bar phrase with the first bar of each phrase restating the motif and the second bar serving as a response. Additionally, check out how bars 6 and 8 are variations of bar 2, clearly employing that theme-and-variation approach from earlier.

The slap part of the groove is fairly conventional and shouldn't present too much of a challenge once you've assimilated the basic technique. If you're experiencing problems, I encourage you to go back and review "The Slap Technique" chapter.

The harmonics in bars 1, 3, 5, and 7 are accomplished by popping—that is, percussively pulling, as is commonly employed in response to the thumb strike when slapping—the harmonics directly above the fifth fret with the right index and middle fingers. This might require a bit of practice on the part of your fretting hand to get used to seamlessly going back and forth between fretting notes and getting the harmonic. It comes together quickly with repetition though.

The chords are double-stops (two notes at a time, right?) accomplished by popping the strings in a manner similar to the aforementioned harmonics, but this time while actually fretting notes.

Once you're feeling comfortable with the part, play along with a metronome and/or drum machine to ensure that the time is solid. Groove hard!

Part 3

As promised, let's dive in this time and comprehensively examine the A-section groove *and* melody from "Blessed" from *Pondering the Sushi* as an actual musical application of weaving various techniques into a single bass part.

Figure 11-9. Exercise 9 (A-section analysis of "Blessed").

All of the basic techniques employed in this example are covered in detail earlier in this book, so please refer back if you have any questions.

As I mentioned in part 1, this song is essentially a bass-and-drum tune. Consequently, bear in mind that as the bass comprises the majority of the sonic space, it's much busier than it would be if a quartet were performing the song.

Let's take a closer look! Don't forget that the sixteenth notes are shuffled, by the way.

Harmonically, the section is basically a G-7 vamp. More specifically, excepting a few passing tones, the entire part implies G Dorian: 1-2-♭3-4-5-6-♭7.

The first two eighth notes are a continuation of the basic groove covered in part 1 of this section. Played using the muted-thumb technique, they establish the groove before jumping to the higher register to play the melody. The melody is played fingerstyle and should be phrased a bit more aggressively and lyrically, as reflected by the vibrato and slides.

The end of the second bar has double-stops or two-note chords that simulate what a guitar might play in an ensemble treatment of this tune.

Bar 3 resumes the groove from the top of the tune, including the slapped line in bar 4. Bar 5 then reestablishes the melodic motif from bar 1, followed by a variation in bar 6. Bar 7 again returns to the groove motif.

By the way, Figure 11-9 includes references to the various effects I employed on the recorded version. While fun, effects aren't critical here; as you'll discover, the technique variations and register jumps already dramatically affect the timbre and create the illusion of multiple voices. But if you have stomp boxes handy, go for it! In the past, I've used a velocity-sensitive envelope filter on the melody when performing this song live.

Get this under your fingers at a slow tempo and you can gradually work it up to speed.

I encourage you to use these examples to launch your own creative explorations into combining different techniques for the purpose of creating fresh and interesting parts.

By the way, any of my examples should be viewed as just that: a possible application of the concept at hand. Always ensure that your own bass lines in real-world situations are in context, and complement and support the song.

Let's Grab Coffee:
Pursuing a Career as a Bassist

I'm frequently approached by Christian bassists seeking input and direction with respect to developing their bass-playing careers and ministries. As a full-time musician, I've pondered and/or wrestled with this topic for years—particularly with some of the facets that challenge the various things I've understood about walking with Christ, abiding, and so on. Some aspects of being a working musician can feel like they conflict with the "Let go and let God"—yes, I'm paraphrasing!—directive of the Scriptures.

The following shouldn't be interpreted as heaven's mandate to every reader. Rather, I'm simply sharing my perspectives and several conclusions that I've reached—in no particular order—through my own personal experiences and time spent seeking God's direction.

It's All About Him

This might sound a bit cliché, but it really is true—in every sense. Whether I'm playing bass, spending time with my family, writing this book, or driving to a session, the only thing that truly matters is whether I'm doing what God wants me to do.

How does that apply to a career in music? At the most fundamental level, pursuing a career as a bassist—or as an attorney, chef, landscaper, or shoe salesperson—absolutely, positively must be something that's only done as a response to God's leading. To put it another way, the *last possible* place you want to be is grinding it out as a starving musician when you know that the Lord has clearly directed you elsewhere.

Theological debates about concepts such as God's *permissive* will versus His *perfect* will definitely go beyond the scope of this book. Suffice it to say that the working musician's life is not what you want to be pursuing unless it's something to which you've been called.

If He *is* leading you, then you're in for the ride of your life: pursue that calling with all that's within you—to His glory.

The "Ho-Dee-Doe" Strategy

I never intended to be a full-time musician. I was perfectly content having a full-time day gig and doing music/ministry very actively on the side. But at a certain point, God made it crystal clear that He was directing me to trade in the security of the day gig for the thrills of faith, self-employment, and full-time music/ministry. Interestingly, years earlier, my very discerning wife informed me that this was coming—to which I responded with much laughter and a speech about the implausibility of it all. God's got a good sense of humor. Thankfully, so does my amazing wife.

Anyway, because I never set out to do this, my entire career has been a constant cycle of God opening doors and me "ho-dee-doe-ing" (is that how that's spelled?) my way through them. Lots of folks inquire about my professional and career strategies, to which I can only say that I don't really have any, nor have I ever. It's all been God.

I'm not saying that people shouldn't think through, plan, or otherwise utilize their cerebral faculties when pursuing goals—whether musical or otherwise—in life, but rather, that those things should always be held with a loose grip. The Lord can and will do absolutely amazing things if we are receptive to His leading—and those things will be infinitely more worthwhile than anything we could devise and strategize on our own.

Diligently Pursue Excellence

Whether your calling is to play on concert stages or in nursing homes, spend time developing and investing in the talents God's given you. Be prepared for the musical opportunities the Lord brings your way. Let Him be glorified through excellence.

Louisville or Los Angeles

From a practical standpoint, if you're sensing a calling toward being a touring musician in Contemporary Christian Music (CCM), you probably need to seriously consider moving to Nashville. There's nothing mysterious about that; it's simply the industry hub and home base for most touring CCM artists. Ironically, Lincoln Brewster was a rare exception, being based in Northern California, but the fact remains that most other artists in the field are based in Nashville.

If you sense your calling is to be a session musician, many regions have some sort of recording scene—although it has dramatically changed with technology, the economy, and the proliferation of home studios—but the biggest towns in the United States with any remnant of a traditional session scene are New York, Nashville, and Los Angeles.

If you feel you're called to be a club musician, then there are local and regional music scenes around the country that may not require quite as much of a transplantation.

It's a good idea to *count the cost*, though, as the bigger the scene, the higher the concentration of scary, scary players shooting for the same opportunities you're pursuing. See "It's All About Him," above!

Light and Salt

As believers out in the music world, many of us grapple with the conflicting values of the business versus the Lord. I'm convinced that we each have a calling and a designated, strategic place, whether that lies in the secular music world, Christian music/ministry environment, or both. By the way, you will likely discover, if you haven't already, that the Christian music biz can regretfully be just as prone to weirdness as its mainstream counterpart.

Regardless of whichever environment God places us in, though, we are called to be light and salt (Matthew 5:13–16). I know that iconic session players Abraham Laboriel and Alex Acuna are tremendous witnesses for the Lord in the secular music scene, both through artistic excellence and really living out their faith. I've heard numerous accounts of them leading their colleagues in the Los Angeles studios to Christ. Isn't that inspiring? God is the best.

My encouragement to you is to seek His direction for you, then proceed with confidence in Him. If that ends up being in Christian music or ministry, awesome; let Him shine through you. If that ends up being in the deepest recesses of the mainstream music biz, awesome again; the Lord might use you to extend love, grace, and hope to those without it. You may very well be the only believer in many of those people's lives. Your lifestyle witness through musical excellence, professionalism, integrity—and genuinely loving and caring for people—will speak volumes. In other words, don't let the sordid elements of the industry weigh you down; be a light in that sphere of your influence by God's grace and leading.

12

Solo Bass Arranging: An Introducion

Everything that's been covered in this book so far has prepared you for this next step! Are you ready to dip your toes into the pool for some solo bass arranging? Before some of you go running from the room, screaming something about "I'm too old to be playing coffee-house gigs," please hear me out—and you're *never* too old to play coffee-house gigs, by the way!

The bass is an amazingly rich and versatile instrument. It's also surprisingly well suited for playing as a solo instrument. But even if that's not your bag, I think it's nonetheless hugely valuable for your musicianship to delve into this area at least a bit, even if just as an educational endeavor. There's something about time spent being involved with all aspects of the musical arrangement—melody, harmony, rhythm, sonics—that can substantially deepen your understanding of music and how ensembles function. It can make you a better bass player, arranger, and producer, and can even enhance your compositional skills.

Getting into a lengthy explanation of arrangement concepts and everything that can possibly go into putting together an unaccompanied bass piece goes beyond this book's scope. But pretty much every concept I've covered—fingerboard familiarity, groove, playing a part, phrasing, technique, and so on—can have direct applicability to putting together a solo bass arrangement of a tune.

Not every piece need be a virtuosic, mind-boggling jazz-reharmonization-from-Mars, by the way. Although that's a fun area to explore down the road, the simple stuff can be really sweet and beautiful too.

Part 1

This excursion into solo bass arranging will focus on the traditional Christmas carol "Angels We Have Heard on High (Gloria)." I'd like to begin by looking at just the melody and harmony of the verse section (Figure 12-1). The actual solo arrangement will be covered after and should make more sense once you have a solid understanding of the piece.

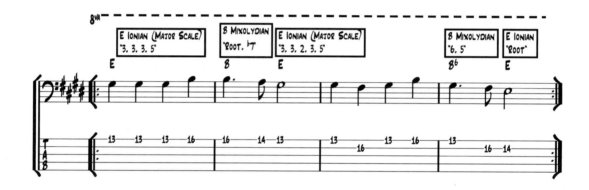

Figure 12-1. Exercise 1 (melodic and harmonic analysis: verse section).

With a bass guitar, it's helpful to put the song in a key where you can take advantage of open strings, as that obviously somewhat lightens the burden on your fretting hand. For this reason, many solo bass arrangements can be found in the keys of E or A, as they allow for melody or chord tones to be voiced on the higher strings while letting a low string ring.

This arrangement will be in the key of E. The basic chord motion will be very simple, alternating back and forth from the I to the V chords. The melody should be a familiar one to most of you; don't forget that 8va indicates the note should be played an octave higher than written. In the text above the staff, you'll see both the default applicable scale and the intervals found in the melody (relative to the underlying chord). Pretty straightforward stuff. If any of this is confusing for you, please refer to the "Suggested Resources" section for help with the modes.

Please take some time to play and assimilate the verse melody. After getting comfortable with it, try playing the root of the chord while playing that melody. Don't worry about trying to make it smooth and "solo-ish"; you'll get to that stuff soon!

Part 2

Now continue on with the first part of the chorus section (Figure 12-2). This should be a really familiar part of the song to most of you; think "Glo-o-o-o-o-O-o-o-o-o-O-o-o-o-o-O-ria . . ."

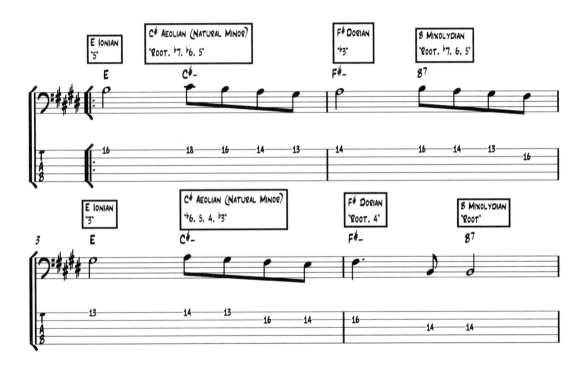

Figure 12-2. Exercise 2 (melodic and harmonic analysis: chorus section).

The basic chord progression will be I–VIm–IIm–V7, a half note per chord. Play through and get this part of the chorus melody under your fingers (beautiful line, isn't it? Wish I'd written it!) After you've assimilated it, try to add the roots of the chords as you play through that melody. Again, we'll work on phrasing and smoothing it out later; just try to get those two elements together. Have a blast!

Part 3

Now for the second part of the chorus section (Figure 12-3). Part 2 covered the familiar "Glooooooooo-ria" part; this will be the "in excelsis Deo" line that follows it.

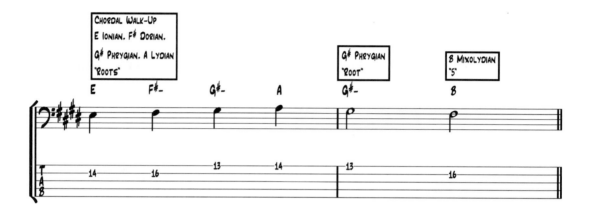

Figure 12-3. Exercise 3 (melodic and harmonic analysis: chorus section).

You'll notice that the chord motion for the first measure is very hymn-esque in its chord-change-every-quarter-note approach. Those of you who are starting to convulse just a bit as you reflect on your lifetime of reading down hymns on Sunday morning while attempting to make them groove: please hang in there! It's actually kind of cool this time—in a traditional-Christmas-tune way.

The second measure resumes the earlier convention of changing chords on the half note. Those of you who've had some experience with arranging will probably notice that the G#m chord you'll be utilizing on those first two beats is commonly an inversion of the I chord (E/G♯) instead. That's the beauty of arranging a piece: you can take some artistic liberties if you are so inclined! I preferred the sound of G♯m in this particular version, but if it irks you, feel free to rebel and create your own version using E/G♯!

Part 4

Before I get into the actual execution of the piece, it will also be helpful to quickly look at the chord voicings and forms around which the melody will be played. I'll isolate the verse section this time (Figure 12-4).

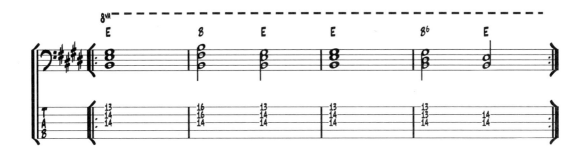

Figure 12-4. Exercise 4 (chord voicings: verse section).

You might recall that the basic chord motion for the verse is I–V. The first bar has an E major chord played with the fifth as the lowest note. The B major chord in the second measure is technically a B5 chord (or *power chord*), as it contains just the root, fifth, and octave. The E major chord on beat 3 returns to the chord form in the first measure.

That progression repeats in bars 3 and 4, with the exception that the B major chord is voiced as a B6 chord in the fourth measure to accommodate the melody.

As always, the 8va indicates that the notes are played an octave higher than written. I always prefer this to dealing with a bunch of ledger lines (as keyboardists and wind players out there scoff loudly!)

Anyway, this is pretty straightforward stuff, but it's important to have a solid understanding of this before combining chords and melody for an actual arrangement.

As I've mentioned before, there are subjective aspects to some of the musical choices involved; I'll explain my choices once I get to the arrangement itself. As you begin your own solo-bass-arranging endeavors, I definitely encourage you to evaluate and make your own artistic decisions as well!

Part 5

Many of the chords in my analysis might seem fragmented or harmonically incomplete, but don't worry: the melody will fill in many of these harmonic holes, and there's a method to the madness!

Last time, I focused on the verse section. Let's now look at the first part of the chorus section (Figure 12-5): "Glo-o-o-o-o-o-o-o-o-o-ria!"

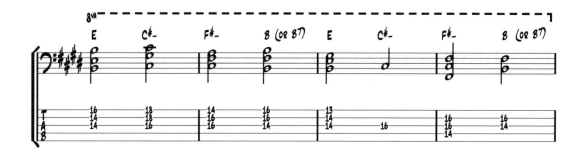

Figure 12-5. Exercise 5 (chord voicings: chorus section).

The chorus progression in this arrangement starts with I–VIm–IIm–V, played twice. As in the verse section, the I chord (E major) is played with the fifth (or B) as the lowest note. This technically makes it an E5 chord, as I'm not including the third on this pass.

As a quick aside, this chord voicing is referred to as the *second inversion*. You can think of inversions as the bass or low note of the chord being a chord tone other than the root note. The first inversion would have been if you played the third (G♯) under that E major chord. Some very cool motion and voice leading can be found in exploring inversions—but always use your musical discernment and taste, as inversions are often best used sparingly.

Anyway, back to the chorus. The VIm chord (C♯ minor) is here voiced as a C♯5 chord too—comprising the root, fifth, and octave. The IIm chord of F♯ minor again employs the second inversion voicing with the fifth (C♯) as the low note. The proceeding V chord (B or B7) is voiced as a B5.

In bar 3, the chord progression repeats. The I chord of E major is again voiced as the second inversion, but is now a true E major, as it includes the third (G♯) on top. Take note of the fact that the VIm chord, C♯ minor, this time is covered by *just* the root (ooooh, cliffhanger! Stay tuned!) The IIm chord (F♯ minor) in bar 4 is played as F♯5 this time, as is the V chord (B5) occurring in the second half of the measure.

Part 6

Lastly, here's a look at the chord voicings and forms of the "in excelsis Deo" part of the chorus (Figure 12-6).

A basic understanding of diatonic harmony will quickly illuminate the chord motion for the first bar as: I–IIm–IIIm–IV. The second measure is IIIm and V—a half note each.

The chord voicings are basic triads containing root, third, and fifth. For the detail oriented among you: yes, all but the last chord are second inversion, played with the fifth of the chord as the lowest note.

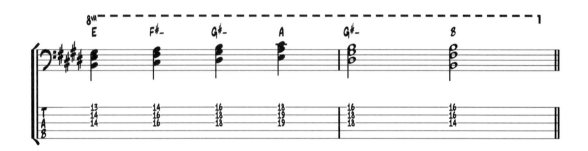

Figure 12-6. Exercise 6 (chord voicings: chorus section).

As I mentioned earlier, I made the artistic choice in this particular arrangement to use the IIIm (G♯ minor) on beat 1 of the second measure versus E/G♯ . Again, feel free to create your own version using the latter if you're so inclined!

Part 7

Having evaluated the harmony, melody, and rhythms, you're now ready to dive in headfirst to the actual execution of this solo bass arrangement! Begin with the verse section (Figure

12-7). As is frequently the case, the transcription makes the part look a bit scarier than it actually is; please don't be intimidated.

If you compare this transcription with the charts from parts 1 and 4 of this chapter (Figures 12-1 and 12-4), you'll find that I'm simply combining the melody and chords that you've already assimilated. The tied notes are just reflecting the fact that you're plucking chords and arpeggiating some of the figures to give motion, subdivision, and accompaniment for the melody. Remember, the bass is 100 percent of the music now, so it's all up to you!

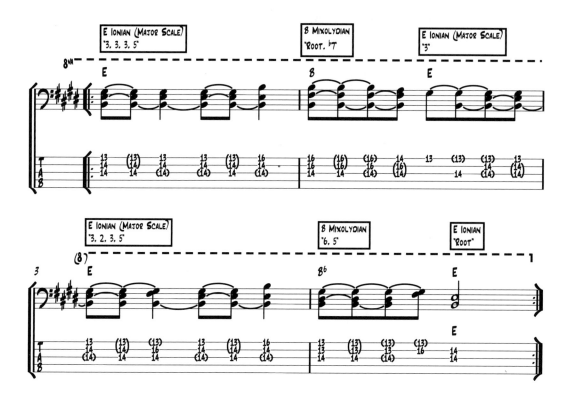

Figure 12-7. Solo bass arrangement (verse section).

Play it as slowly as you need to, and it will start coming together after a few passes. By the way, this entire arrangement only involves fingerstyle technique and plucking. I generally use my thumb for the low string and my index and middle fingers for the higher parts. You'll notice that this arrangement is well suited for a one-finger-per-string approach with the plucking hand—that is, thumb on the A string, index finger on the D string, middle finger on the G string, and so on. For this manner of chordal playing, you'll want to ensure that your plucking fingers don't rake into and inadvertently mute a lower string that is supposed to be sustaining through the passage.

Part 8

Now it's time to proceed with the first four measures of the chorus (Figure 12-8).

   Again, let me emphasize that transcribing this sort of playing accurately can make the part look a bit intimidating on paper. Don't let it throw you; the actual part is really quite simple. Comparing these transcriptions with the charts from parts 2 and 5 of this series (Figures 12-2 and 12-5) will reveal that I'm just combining the melody and chords that have already been covered. All of the rest of it is simply plucking chords and arpeggios to give the piece some motion; think of it as the groove supporting the melody and harmony. Play it slowly, and work it up to speed once you've assimilated it, okay? Have fun!

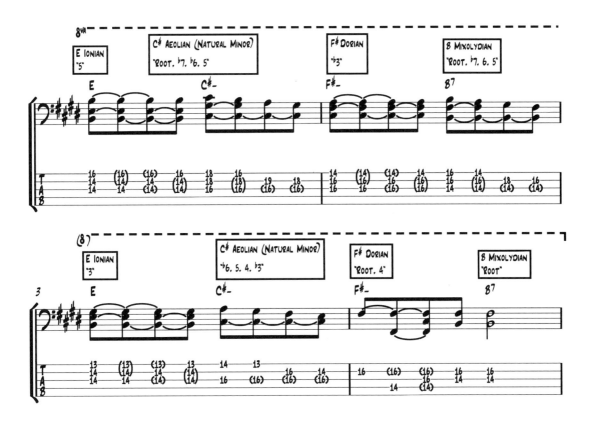

Figure 12-8. Solo bass arrangement (chorus section).

Part 9

Congratulations on making it to the final part of this introduction to solo bass arranging! I hope you've found exploring the harmonic, melodic, and rhythmic aspects of a piece of music to be both illuminating and fun.

Let's look at the second part of the chorus section: the "in excelsis Deo" part (Figure 12-9).

Compare this transcription with the charts from parts 3 and 6 of this chapter (Figures 12-3 and 12-6); it's just a merging of the two. As before, the tied notes make the piece seem intimidating but are simply reflecting that you're plucking chords and arpeggiating some of the figures to provide motion and support for the melody.

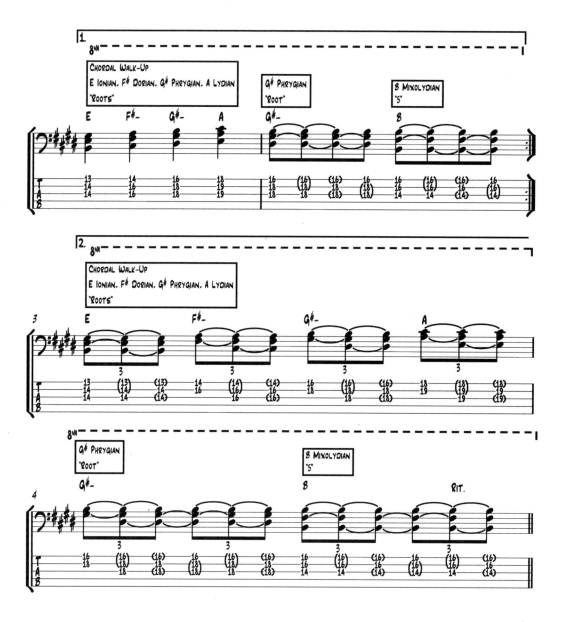

Figure 12-9. Solo bass arrangement (chorus section).

Note that the first staff (bars 1 and 2) is the first ending, so repeat back to the first half of the chorus from Figure 12-8; then play the second ending (bars 3 and 4). For the overly observant, you'll probably notice that there wasn't a start repeat sign at the beginning of the chart last time; I just didn't want to create confusion with the absence of an end repeat sign. Feel free to write one in now!

The only new element is that I've given a couple of different options for the final chord (Figure 12-10); give each a try and pick the one you prefer.

I generally like the harmonic interest resulting from *not* resolving on the tonic or I chord as reflected in option 1, so would lean toward option 2 and ending on the IV chord. But again, it's your call!

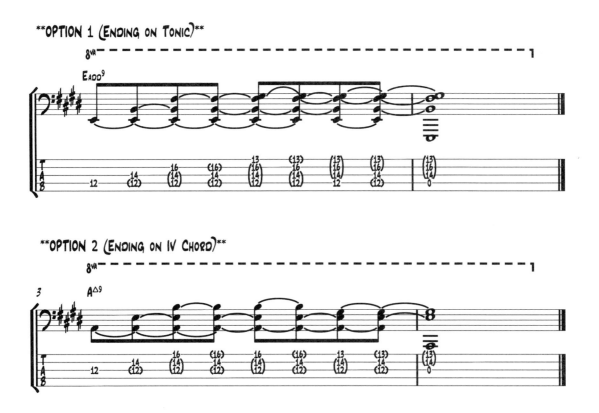

Figure 12-10. Solo bass arrangement (alternate endings).

Let me bring everything together to wrap this up; here's the full arrangement (Figure 12-11).

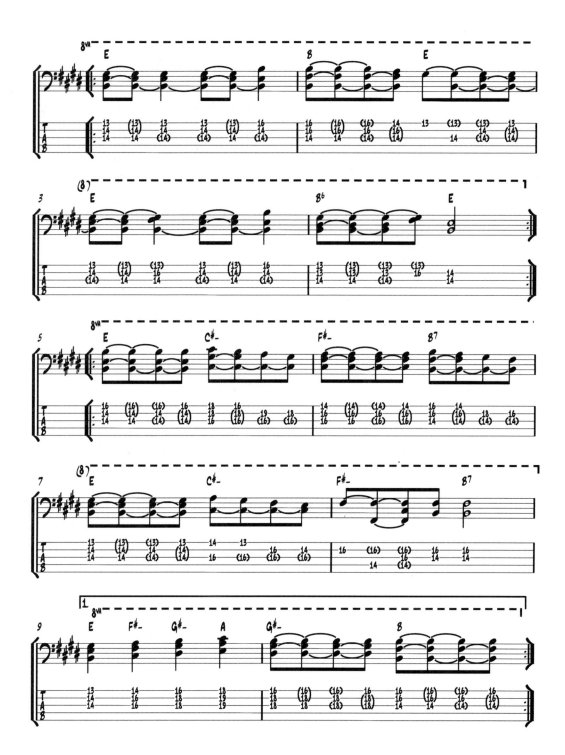

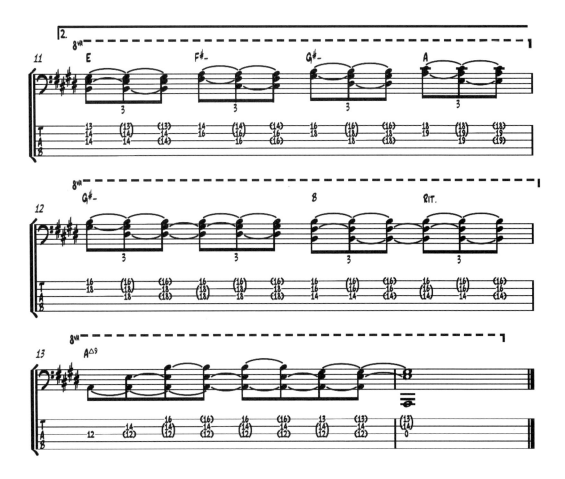

Figure 12-11. Complete performance of solo bass arrangement.

I hope you are inspired to take a stab at working up your own solo bass arrangement. It doesn't have to be anything virtuosic. Just find the melody on your fretboard (ideally in a key that allows use of some of the open strings in your bass accompaniment), identify a practical way to cover the root motion under that melody, and if you're up for it (yes, you are!), try to throw in some chordal accompaniment as you're able. Again, whether or not you ever perform this stuff in public, this will pay big dividends in your overall understanding of music.

A friendly word of caution: you just might discover when all is said and done that it's also an absolute blast!

13

Developing Your Inner Clock

When doing bass clinics or teaching at conferences, I frequently mention that it's my goal to help attendees learn important musical concepts more easily than I did. Throughout my earlier years of being a musician, I often focused on the flashy stuff at the exclusion of solid, foundational playing. Consequently, I only came to appreciate the importance and relevance of many critical aspects of musicianship the hard way—like in the middle of recording sessions!

Perhaps the single most important revelation in this regard had to do with timekeeping. I came to realize that, at the end of the day, no amount of chops or flash could substitute for rhythmically accurate bass playing. There simply is no more critical aspect of our playing than the rhythmic component—and I'm saying this as someone who has a huge appreciation for the melodic and harmonic aspects of bass playing. But rhythm is *job one*.

I immediately began consistently working with a metronome. My perspective changed from bass *guitar* (emphasis on the latter with all manner of noodling and licks) to *bass as drum* (that is, the bass as part of the drum kit).

The good news is that one doesn't need to be born with good time; it can be developed through regular practice with a click.

It should be mentioned that *grooving*, in the context of playing actual music with other musicians, can vary significantly in the degree to which it is metronomic—based upon the musical genre, the desired musical feel, and so on. However, I've found that the starting point is "calibrating" our internal sense of time through consistent work with a metronome.

This allows us to become familiar with how a steady tempo sounds and feels, as well as to recognize our own rhythmic tendencies—for instance, do we tend to rush, or to drag, or are we prone to speeding up when the dynamic level builds and/or slowing down when the dynamic level drops, and so on.

To that end, let's spend some time focusing on developing timekeeping. For each exercise in this chapter, you'll be working with two rhythmic figures for the metronome clicks (Figure 13-1).

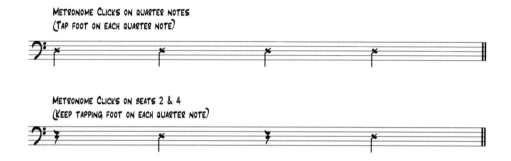

Figure 13-1. Metronome clicks.

The top staff reflects the usual convention of clicks on the quarter notes (think, "one, two, three, four . . ."). As the note in Figure 13-1 indicates, get used to tapping your foot on each quarter note. The second staff reflects the click on just beats 2 and 4 and can be accomplished easily by reducing the bpm to half of the original tempo.

Part 1

Beginning with the click playing the top staff of Figure 13.1 (quarter notes), play through Exercises 1A and 1B (Figure 13-2).

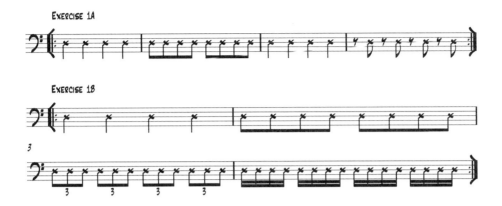

Figure 13-2. Exercises 1A and 1B.

Again, be sure to tap your foot with the metronome and try to internalize the tempo. Also watch your foot in measure 4 of Exercise 1A: it should still be tapping on the downbeats, with the notes being played on the upbeats. The key is to keep the quarter-note foot tapping constant regardless of the rhythmic figure being played.

You'll notice that Exercises 1C and 1D are simply the first two exercises played with string skipping (Figure 13-3).

Figure 13-3. Exercises 1C and 1D.

Just mute the strings with your fretting hand and pluck the strings as indicated. Don't worry, pitch will be added later; for now, focus on rhythmic accuracy and avoiding flamming with the click. The sound of the click should disappear when you're locking with it. If possible, record yourself repetitively playing these exercises and listen back critically for flams.

Once these feel comfortable, try to play them again with the metronome playing the second staff in Figure 13-1—just beats 2 and 4—while maintaining your foot taps on each quarter note. This click placement helps create the feeling of backbeat a drummer's snare drum would typically provide.

Practice these at a variety of tempos. You might be surprised to find how challenging it is to play these accurately at slower tempos—say, 60 bpm and slower. Don't shy away from them; some of the best rhythmic practice and *inner clock calibration* happens at those slower bpms.

Part 2

Now play through Exercises 2A–2D (Figure 13-4). Once again, you'll be using a click playing the rhythmic figures from Figure 13-1.

Figure 13-4. Exercises 2A–2D.

Start with clicks on each quarter note. A good starting tempo is 90 bpm.

Exercise 2A might seem like a step back in rhythmic progression from where you've been, but the point of these exercises is to develop your internal sense of time, which needs to be accurate through an array of subdivisions. In fact, you might find it harder to play this exercise accurately—that is, flam-free—than some of the busier ones.

As before, make sure you tap your foot with the metronome and try to internalize the tempo and subdivisions—paying particular attention to your foot wherever the figure departs from the downbeat, as in the third bar of Exercise 2A or end of second bar of Exercise 2B. Your foot should still be tapping on the quarter notes regardless of the rhythmic figure being played.

Once you've acclimated, play 2A–2D again with the metronome playing the second figure from Figure 13-1—just the backbeats—while maintaining your foot taps on each downbeat. Practice these at a variety of tempos.

Part 3

I hope this focus on developing and calibrating your internal sense of time is proving helpful. On a tangential note, you might also have noticed the multitasking here: in addition to working on your timekeeping and subdivision, this series also is a fairly intensive primer for sight-reading rhythms! Isn't it great when you can develop multiple areas of your musicianship concurrently?

Play through Exercises 3A–3J (Figure 13-5) with the click playing those quarter notes at 90 bpm, slowing down a bit if needed, and then work through them again while the click is playing just backbeats.

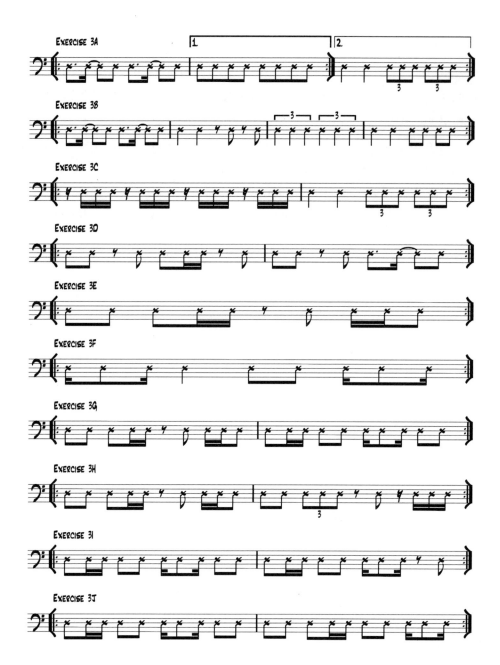

Figure 13-5. Exercises 3A–3J.

Here's that list of things to keep in mind. To avoid redundancy, it won't appear in subsequent lessons, but please refer back to it here. Suffice it to say that it applies to the rest of the exercises in this chapter.

- Feel free to spend a moment getting the exercise in your ears and under your fingers without the click. Then play it with the metronome—first with the click on quarter notes, then eventually on just the backbeats (see Figure 13-1).
- Listen intently for flams (two distinct, nearly simultaneous hits) resulting from your note not occurring precisely with the click. See if you can play each exercise flam free. Record yourself, and listen back critically.
- Don't take the repeats literally. Play each figure as many times as it takes to really internalize it—and then play it some more! The focus isn't as much on successfully executing the line as it is on calibrating your inner clock.
- Make sure to tap your foot on the quarter notes and assimilate both the tempo and how the various subdivisions feel over those quarter notes. Ensure that your foot doesn't depart from those downbeats, regardless of the rhythmic figure being played or metronome figure used.
- Once the exercise is coming together, practice it at a variety of tempos; the slower tempos can be surprising challenging to play accurately.
- Play the exercises while dynamically alternating between loud and quiet, gradually getting louder or quieter over the course of several repeats, striving to keep the rhythmic accuracy regardless of dynamic level.

Part 4

Are you well on your way to getting extremely comfortable with the click? I hope so. This really is crucial stuff for your musicianship—and *so* worth the investment of time and effort.

One of the common traits of really groove-oriented players is that they internalize the subdivision of the groove, whether they're actually playing those subdivisions or not. They can play a really syncopated and busy line or a relatively simple and legato part, yet any embellishments or variations they play are completely lined up with the underlying subdivision or grid.

This idea will be explored with Exercises 4A–4D (Figure 13-6).

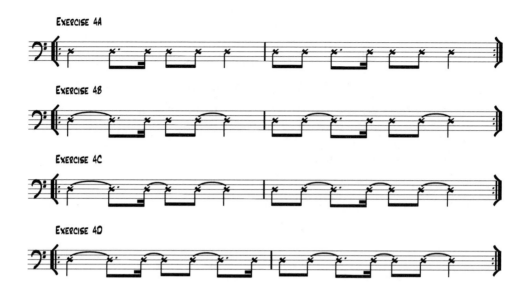

Figure 13-6. Exercises 4A–4D.

If you look at Exercise 4A, you'll see a fairly straightforward rhythmic motif. Comparing the first and second measures of the phrase, it's quickly apparent that they're identical except for the added eighth note on the *and* of beat 1.

Exercises 4B and 4C are the same rhythmic motif, but with some of the notes tied together. For those of you who are new to reading, simply let the first note sustain through the tied note as well; don't pluck it on the tied note.

Exercise 4D is almost identical, except for the added sixteenth note right before beat 1 of the second measure.

These exercises imply an underlying sixteenth-note subdivision, although neither the click nor the majority of the line do. If you can internalize that subdivision as you're playing these, you'll be well on your way.

Please refer back to part 3 for that list of things to keep in mind!

Part 5

Up till now, you might have been feeling like there wasn't a lot of applicability between the practice exercises and real-world groove playing. The following exercises (Figure 13-7) will establish some relevance!

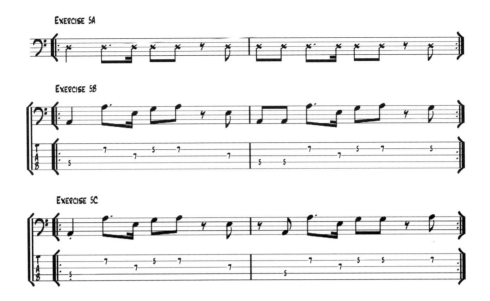

Figure 13-7. Exercises 5A–5C.

Exercise 5A reflects a very minor tweak of the basic rhythmic figure involved in the exercises from last time (Figure 13-6); the only difference is the hit on beat 4 has been displaced by an eighth note to the *and* of beat 4.

Let's give pitch to this rhythmic figure. Exercise 5B reflects a bass line that would work well under an A-7 or A7 vamp. Exercise 5C introduces some minor but fun variations to 5B.

Play through Exercises 5A–5C with the click playing on the quarter notes at 100 bpm—again, slow down a bit if needed—and then work through them again while the click is playing just those backbeats. See part 3 for the list.

After you get comfortable playing with the click, set up a basic eighth-note drum groove at 100 bpm and play these exercises to it. The drum pattern will likely be easier to lock with, as it provides more subdivision than the click.

Part 6

Let's continue charging ahead in full *practical application* mode. The exercises in Figure 13-8 simply add pitch and phrasing to the basic rhythmic practice figures from earlier in the chapter, making only occasional minor tweaks and revealing actual usable bass lines!

By the way, although you're working on several aspects of your musicianship at once—sight-reading, timekeeping, technical execution of the bass line, musical phrasing, and so on—please don't lose sight of the primary focus of rhythmic accuracy.

Figure 13-8. Exercises 6A–6D.

Exercise 6A is the same rhythmic figure used in part 5 (Figure 13-7) last time. As you may recall, it's a two-bar phrase, although the only difference between the two measures is the added eighth note on the *and* of beat 1 of bar 2.

Exercise 6B basically gives pitch to that rhythmic figure but extends the phrase with a variation in bar 4. The slide off of the last note in bar 3 sets up that bit of air in the line and can give the part a bit of attitude if phrased lazily. The overall part involves a bit of harmonic tension and release with the chromatic walk-up from D to E, which could be effective in a funk rock or R&B context.

If you compare the rhythmic motif of Exercise 6C with that in 6A, you'll see they're quite similar; the primary difference is the rest on the downbeat of beat 2. Isn't it interesting how such a minor difference can have such a profound effect on the feel of the rhythm? To my ear, Exercise 6C sets up a much sparser musical statement.

Exercise 6D gives pitch to the rhythmic figure in 6C, while taking some liberty in the fourth measure. This bass line also leans toward the funk rock or R&B genres, and gives you an opportunity to work on your timekeeping while also focusing on making the part *talk*! Music is about emotive communication, right?

For overachievers out there who might be curious about the harmony of the bass line in Exercise 6D: suffice it to say that it incorporates E Dorian—refer to "Suggested Resources" for more on the modes—and does imply a chord motion to D and A7 in the second and fourth measures. The *tritones* (notes that are three whole steps apart, such as the C♯ and G in the second ending) also inject a bit of funkiness.

As before, play through these exercises with the click falling on the quarter notes at 100 bpm, or slower if needed, then work through them again while the click is playing just backbeats. The watch list is back in part 3.

Once you get comfortable playing with the click, fire up that basic eighth-note drum groove at 100 bpm and play these exercises to it. Groove hard!

Part 7

I'll wrap up this chapter with another example (Figure 13-9) that brings together practice-time rudiments with real-world application!

Figure 13-9. Exercises 7A–7C.

Exercise 7A contains rhythmic groupings with which you should be familiar by now. Hum and/or play through this measure a few times to assimilate it.

Exercise 7B establishes the rhythm for the bass line. A quick comparison between 7A and 7B reflects that the underlying rhythmic groupings are identical—some of the notes are just tied together—excepting a minor variation in the first part of the second ending (bar 4 when the exercise is played as written).

Exercise 7C gives pitch to the rhythms of 7B. In my mind, I was hearing this bass line in a medium-tempo rock setting—a bit more of a riff-conducive context—possibly with a bit of overdrive in the tone. Some of the note choices are idiomatic of modern-rock bass playing, as they alternate between harmonic tension and resolution.

By the way, I didn't specify phrasing because context would have so much to do with it. In the scenario I described above, I would definitely be inclined to incorporate a few slides and slurs to help emote the part, particularly when sliding up from C to E at beat 3 of the second ending. On the other hand, this line could work on a P-bass in a vibey, slow shuffle groove with a singer-songwriter and acoustic guitar—in which case it might be cool and a little funkier to replace the tied note on the downbeat of beat 2 with a quick rest. What do you think? Let your musical taste and discernment lead the way!

As before, play the exercises at 100 bpm—or slow down a bit if needed, then gradually work up to that tempo. Once they're solid with the click, play them with that basic eighth-note drum groove. Please refer back to the list in part 3.

There are so many fun and creative things that can be done on the bass guitar both melodically and harmonically, but making regular calibration of your internal sense of time a top priority will serve you well. I hope you'll make these sorts of exercises a permanent part of your woodshed time. God bless you and your *groove ministry*!

14

Coda: A Grace Case's Perspective

Let me start by expressing my profound gratitude to you for having joined me on this journey! I sincerely hope this material proves helpful for your ongoing growth as a musician in general and worship bassist in particular.

I'd like to conclude our time with some closing thoughts and encouragement about ministry, art, and matters of the heart.

Throne Check

If you're reading this book, you might spend a fair amount of your time and energy serving in your church's worship ministry. God bless you—and thank you for investing your life and talents toward directing the eyes of the church to the Lord. That's a huge deal.

As a musician, it's the highest possible calling, isn't it? This music literally has *eternal significance*—intrinsically. It's pretty humbling when you really think about it, and that calling comes with big responsibility.

We have a responsibility to regularly conduct "throne checks"—of our hearts—to ensure that we haven't wiggled our way up there and nudged God aside. Let's never allow ourselves to play Christian on Sunday morning and live self-absorbed and carnal lives the rest of the week.

Please don't misunderstand: we're all "grace cases." His mercies were new this morning and will be new again tomorrow morning (Lamentations 3:22–23). Our failures—past, present, and future—were nailed to the cross with Christ. But I want to *encourage* you—and *remind* myself—that the bottom line with authentic faith is not rules and regulations, but a relationship with God. Let's take that relationship seriously and be real with Him.

Perspective Alignment

I don't mean to offend anyone, but the fact of the matter is that God could easily make a really amazing bass player out of…a compost pile, right? It's an enormous privilege that He allows us to be involved. So let's "walk humbly with our God," as the Scripture says.

I also encourage you to occasionally read—and re-read—the fifth chapter of Revelation. Try to imagine the worship scene John describes. It's pretty overwhelming stuff, to say the least. Really good for reestablishing a proper perspective on what it's all about.

Be That Guy (or Girl)

Love, encourage, honor, and serve the rest of your band (*man, that's not something we'd have gone for in the old days, huh?*); it's the coolest thing ever. The tightness and community that develop in a group when everyone is laying it down for one another are not to be missed.

Be a pillar in the team—musically, spiritually, relationally—someone that can be relied upon, confided in, and otherwise trusted to always have God's best in mind for everyone involved.

Wild Abandon

Imagination and creativity are things to be diligently pursued; they bear testimony to the Lord's creative genius and the talents He's graciously given. Let's pursue originality, artistic integrity, and musical excellence with wild abandon—to God's glory.

Relentless Learning

Whether you've been playing for 30 years or 30 minutes, strive to remain a student, continually seeking to learn and to further develop. Music, much like our spiritual lives, seems to be one of those "the more I learn the more I discover there is to learn" endeavors. May the Lord continue to ignite that desire in each of us to grow.

Grace

God is a gracious God. It's quite overwhelming when I consider the road the Lord's brought me down since that day back in 1989 when I rededicated myself to Christ. Out of the smoldering ruins following eight years of trying to do it my way, He began an unbelievable and ongoing work of redemption in every facet of my life.

I would like to encourage you this day to entrust Him with every aspect of your life. He is good, and He is faithful.

Appendix A: About the DVD-ROM

About the DVD-ROM

The accompanying DVD-ROM includes assorted audio and video clips (and one chart PDF) to support various musical examples and exercises in this book. Many were recorded exclusively for this book, while some are excerpted from either the *Grooving for Heaven* DVD series, my *Pondering the Sushi* and *Tea in the Typhoon* instrumental CDs, or curriculum at ArtOfGroove.com. A handful of the musical examples feature preset accompaniment from my vintage and trusty Roland PMA-5 or Apple's GarageBand. The live musicians featured on the recorded examples include David Owens and Frank Reina on drums, Aaron Redfield on percussion, Rob Rinderer and Kamau Kenyatta on keys, and Joel Whitley on guitar.

1. Figure 2.1. C major scale.*
2. Figure 2.2. Octave Shape 1 practice.*
3. Figure 2.3. Octave Shape 2 practice.*
4. Figure 2.5. C natural minor scale.*
5. Figure 2.6. C Mixolydian mode.*
6. Figure 3.1. Ghost-note practice.*
7. Figure 3.2. A major scale with ghost notes.
8. Figure 3.3. Groove without ghost notes.
9. Figure 3.4. Groove with ghost notes.*
10. Figure 3.5. Lick without slurs or hammers.
11. Figure 3.6. Lick with slurs and hammers.
12. Figure 6.1. Country.
13. Figure 6.2. Jazz.
14. Figure 6.3. Swing eighth notes.

15.   Figure 6.4. Funk.

16.   Figure 6.5. Funk vamp.

17.   Figure 6.6. Latin.

18.   Figure 6.7. Reggae.

19.   Figure 6.8. Shuffled sixteenth notes.

20.   Figure 6.9. Rock.

21.   Figure 6.10. Hybrid.

22.   Figure 6.11. Hybrid vamp.

23.   Figure 6.12. Hybrid riff.

24.   Figure 7.1. "Imaginary Tune" rhythm chart.

25.   Figure 8.1. Slap Exercise 1.*

26.   Figure 8.2. Slap Exercise 2.*

27.   Figure 8.3. Slap Exercise 3.*

28.   Figure 8.5. Slap Exercise 5.*

29.   Figure 8.7. Slap Exercise 7.*

30.   Figure 8.9. Slap Exercise 9.*

31.   Figure 8.11. Slap Exercise 11.*

32.   Figure 8.14. Slap Exercise 14.*

33.   Figure 8.16. Slap Exercise 16.*

34.   Figure 8.19. Slap Exercise 19.*

35.   Figure 8.22. Slap Exercise 22: R&B ballad.

36.   Figure 8.23. Slap Exercise 23: Gospel groove.

37.   Figure 8.24. Slap Exercise 24: Funk shuffle.

38.   Figure 8.26. Slap Exercise 26: Bridge from "Pondering the Sushi."

39.   Figure 10.1. Tap Exercise 1.*

40.   Figure 10.3. Tap Exercise 3.*

41.   Figure 10.4. Tap Exercise 4.*

42.   Figure 10.7. Tap Exercise 7.*

43.   Figure 10.8. Tap Exercise 8.

44.   Figure 11.1. Exercise 1: Artificial harmonic.*

45.   Figure 11.3. Exercise 3: Artificial harmonics.*

46.   Figure 11.5. Exercise 5: Muted thumb.*

47.   Figure 11.7. Exercise 7: Excerpt from "Blessed."*

48.   Figure 11.9. Exercise 9: A-section analysis of "Blessed."

*Video clip.

Appendix B: Suggested Resources

Norm's Instructional DVDs*

- *Grooving for Heaven, Volume 1*
- *Grooving for Heaven, Volume 2*
- *The Art of Groove: Taking Your Bass/Drum Relationship to the Next Level* (Grooving, Volume 3)
- *Pondering Bass Technique: From Bass Pyrotechnics to Art* (Grooving, Volume 4)

*Much of the material in this book was adapted from the curriculum in this instructional DVD series.

Norm's Instructional Website (The Art of Groove)
www.ArtOfGroove.com

Sixty-lesson groove course, HD-quality streaming and download lesson clips, song tutorials, and much more. Includes:
- Groove "Bassics": specifically for new bassists.
- Song tutorials for both Norm's acclaimed CDs and Lincoln Brewster's hits.
- Seven hours of *Grooving for Heaven* DVD curriculum.
- Real-World Perspectives: insight and advice from some of the world's best.
- Typhoon Sessions: behind-the-scenes footage from the making of Norm's *Tea in the Typhoon* CD, featuring John Patitucci, Gregg Bissonette, Michael Manring, and many others.

"I Need Specific Help With . . ."

Here's where to go for further in-depth study on some of the topics in this book.

Modes and Diatonic Harmony

- *Grooving for Heaven, Volume 2* DVD
- Level 1 of 60-Lesson Groove Course (ArtOfGroove.com)

Musical Genres

- *Grooving for Heaven, Volume 3* DVD
- Level 3 of 60-Lesson Groove Course (ArtOfGroove.com)

Slap Technique

- *Grooving for Heaven, Volume 2* DVD (beginning–intermediate)
- *Pondering Bass Technique* DVD (intermediate–advanced)
- Tutorial clips for Norm's songs (ArtOfGroove.com)

Other Resources

Much bass-related information can be found at Norm's website: **www.NormStockton.com**.
   Other recommended resources:
- *Funkifying the Clave* by Lincoln Goines and Robbie Ameen (DVD)
- *John Patitucci: Electric Bass 1* (DVD)
- *John Patitucci: Electric Bass 2* (DVD)
- *Randy Jackson: Mastering the Groove* (DVD)
- *The Latin Bass Book* by Oscar Stagnaro (Book/CD)

Index

Worship Musician!™
PRESENTS
Series

Tips for Tight Teams
High-Performance Help for Today's Worship Musician
by Sandy Hoffman

Tips for Tight Teams instructs and equips today's worship musician to function on the musical, relational, and technical levels expected of 21st-century worship team leaders and members. Rooted in Sandy Hoffman's "Ten Top Tips for Tight Teams" curriculum, the book covers a myriad of timeless and relevant worship topics. The goal of *Tips for Tight Teams* is to elevate skill levels to the point where the worship team is no longer a distraction to the people it endeavors to lead into worship.

$16.99 • 8-1/2" x 11" • 160 pages • Softcover
978-1-4584-0291-2

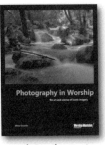

Photography in Worship
The Art and Science of Iconic Imagery
by Mike Overlin

The ability to take a photograph – to stop a moment in time – is a very powerful act in and of itself. When this skill is used in the creation of imagery in support of worship, or even as an act of worship, it can be truly breathtaking. This book will teach you the basics of photography through simple explanations and practical examples, and more important, how to "see" the image in advance, with special emphasis on creating imagery for use in worship.

$29.99 • 8-1/2" x 11" • 208 pages • Softcover
978-1-4584-0295-0

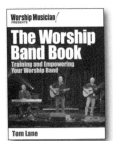

The Worship Band Book
Training and Empowering Your Worship Band
by Tom Lane

Whether you're in a band yourself or part of a ministry involved with teams, this book can help you on your journey. Spiritual, relational, professional, and practical issues relevant for individuals and groups in worship ministry of any kind are addressed head-on. This book will help lay the foundation for a healthier pursuit of creative dreams and a closer walk with God.

$16.99 • 8-1/2" x 11" • 128 pages • Softcover
978-1-4584-1817-3

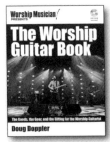

The Worship Guitar Book
The Goods, the Gear, and the Gifting for the Worship Guitarist
by Doug Doppler

Let Doug Doppler demonstrate practice and rehearsal techniques that can mold you into an excellent guitarist while showing you how to blend high musical standards with a heart that's pure and ready to worship God. *The Worship Guitar Book* is written to help the worship team guitarist play better, get great sounds, and function with a good personal and spiritual attitude. Doppler sheds light on the importance of well-designed practice routines, music theory, and working with a team toward a shared intention of supporting a powerful worship experience for the church body.

$19.99 • 8-1/2" x 11" • 312 pages • Softcover w/DVD-ROM
978-1-4584-9120-6

The Worship Drum Book
Concepts to Empower Excellence
by Carl Albrecht

This is a powerful guide for drummers in contemporary churches and for drummers in traditional churches who are making the transition from worship supported by organ or piano to worship supported by a full rhythm section. It addresses important traditional drumming techniques and concepts, while also explaining the unique role that drummers – or musicians of any sort – have as minstrels in the house of the Lord.

$19.99 • 8-1/2" x 11" • 160 pages • Softcover w/DVD-ROM
978-1-4768-1415-5

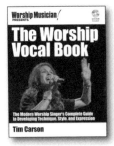

The Worship Vocal Book
The Modern Worship Singer's Complete Guide to Developing Technique, Style, and Expression
by Tim Carson

Author Tim Carson has been traveling the country, helping singers of all types learn to present themselves and their music. At a wide range of conferences and sessions, the principles presented in *The Worship Vocal Book* have proven to produce better singers, time and time again. The techniques in this book draw on four hundred years of classical, foundational vocal instruction and yet they are fresh. Carson presents them in a way that is different from any other method available today, particularly as it pertains to the contemporary worship singer, leader, songwriter, or performer.

$19.99 • 8-1/2" x 11" • 168 pages • Softcover w/DVD-ROM
978-1-4584-4320-5

HAL•LEONARD®

Prices, contents, and availability subject to change without notice.